STRANGE EVENTS COLORING BOOK

BY ERIC FELDERMAN

Books by Eric Felderman

The Riddle of the Universe Solved! (With 37 Misleading Pictures)

The Sins of Santa Claus

Vain Bibble Babble

Shakespeare Corrected and Improved

Ecclesiastes Variations

Animal Book

(and others)

STRANGE EVENTS COLORING BOOK

BY

ERIC FELDERMAN

KDP

ericfelderman23@yahoo.com

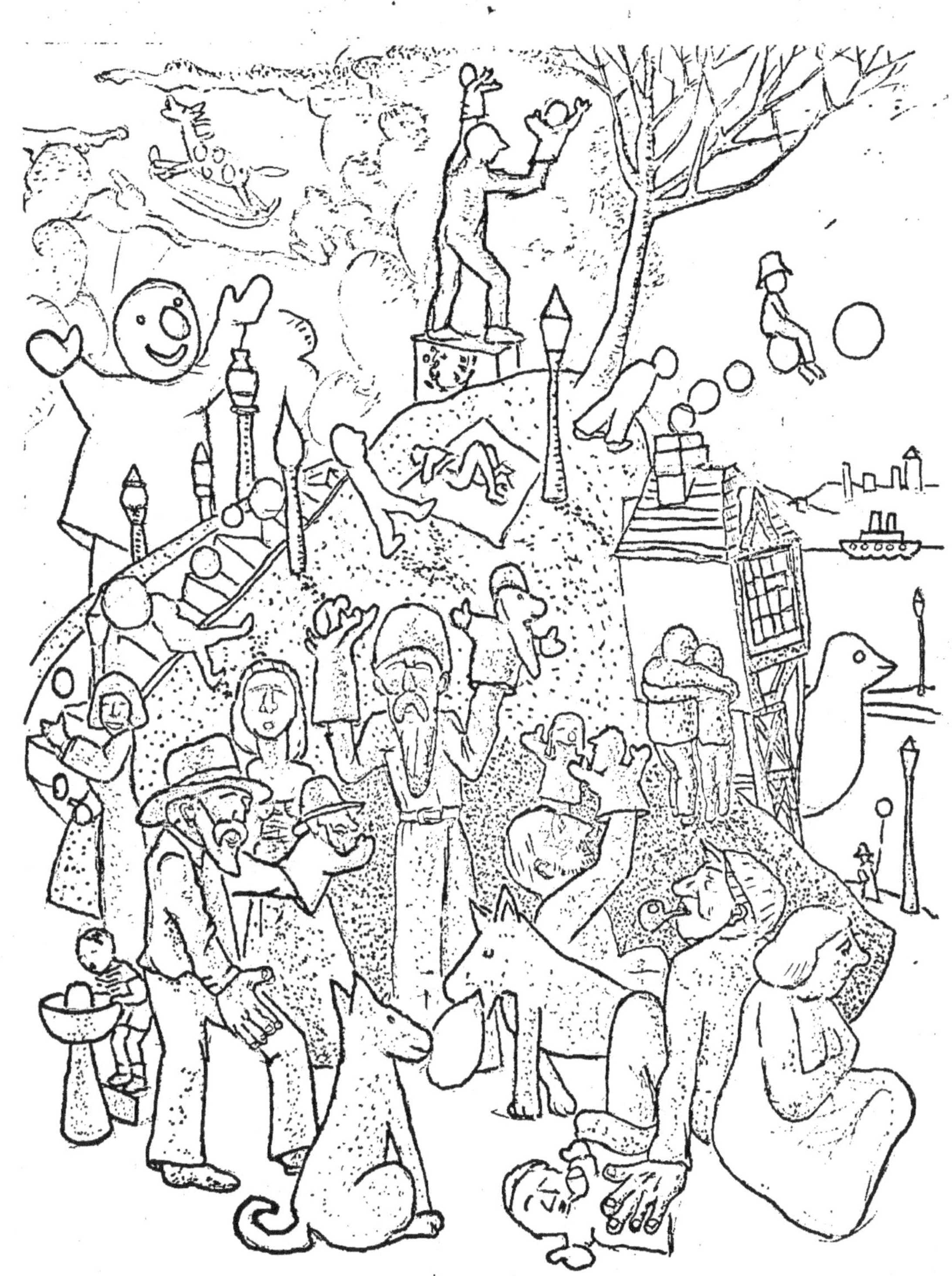

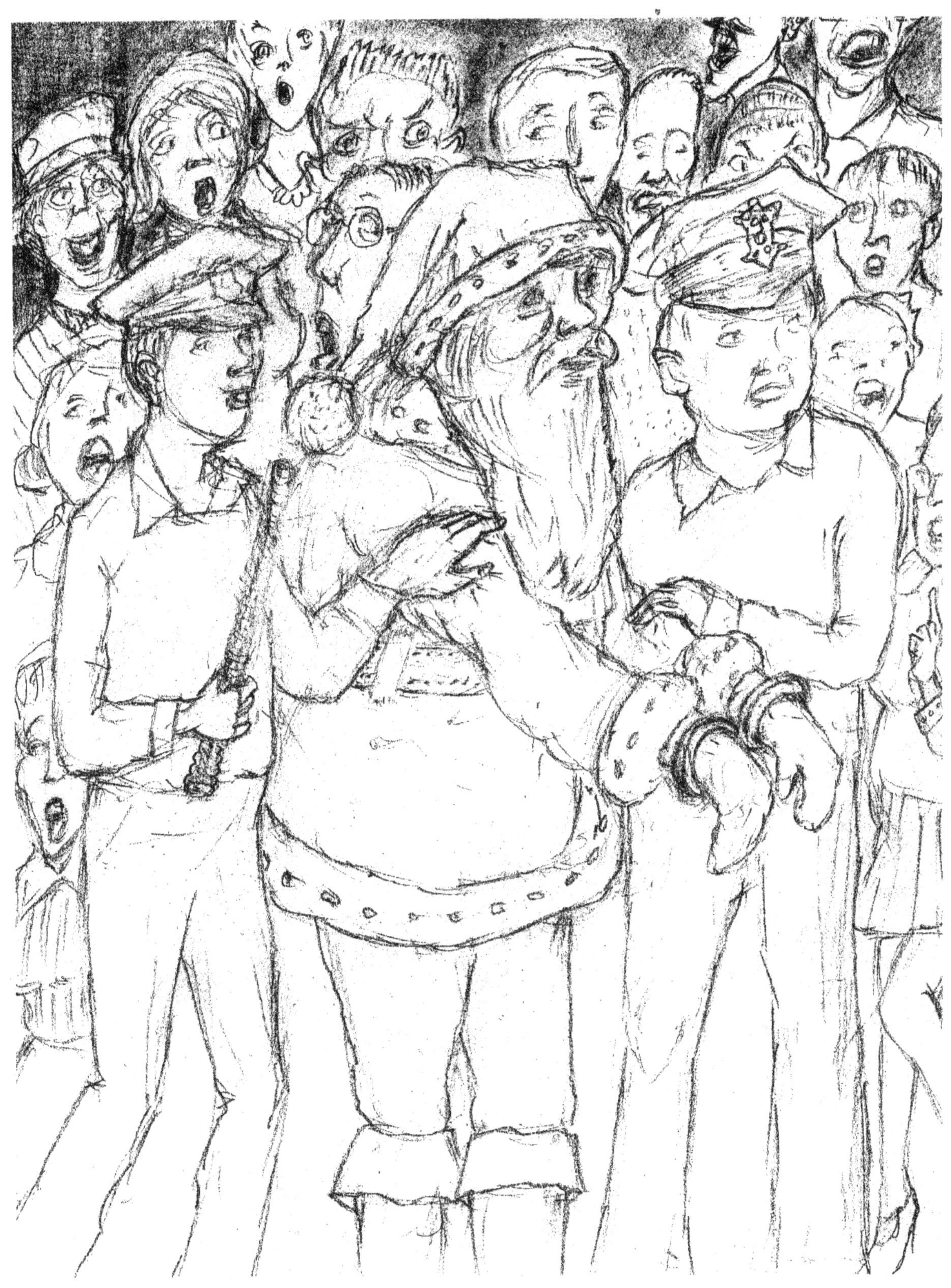

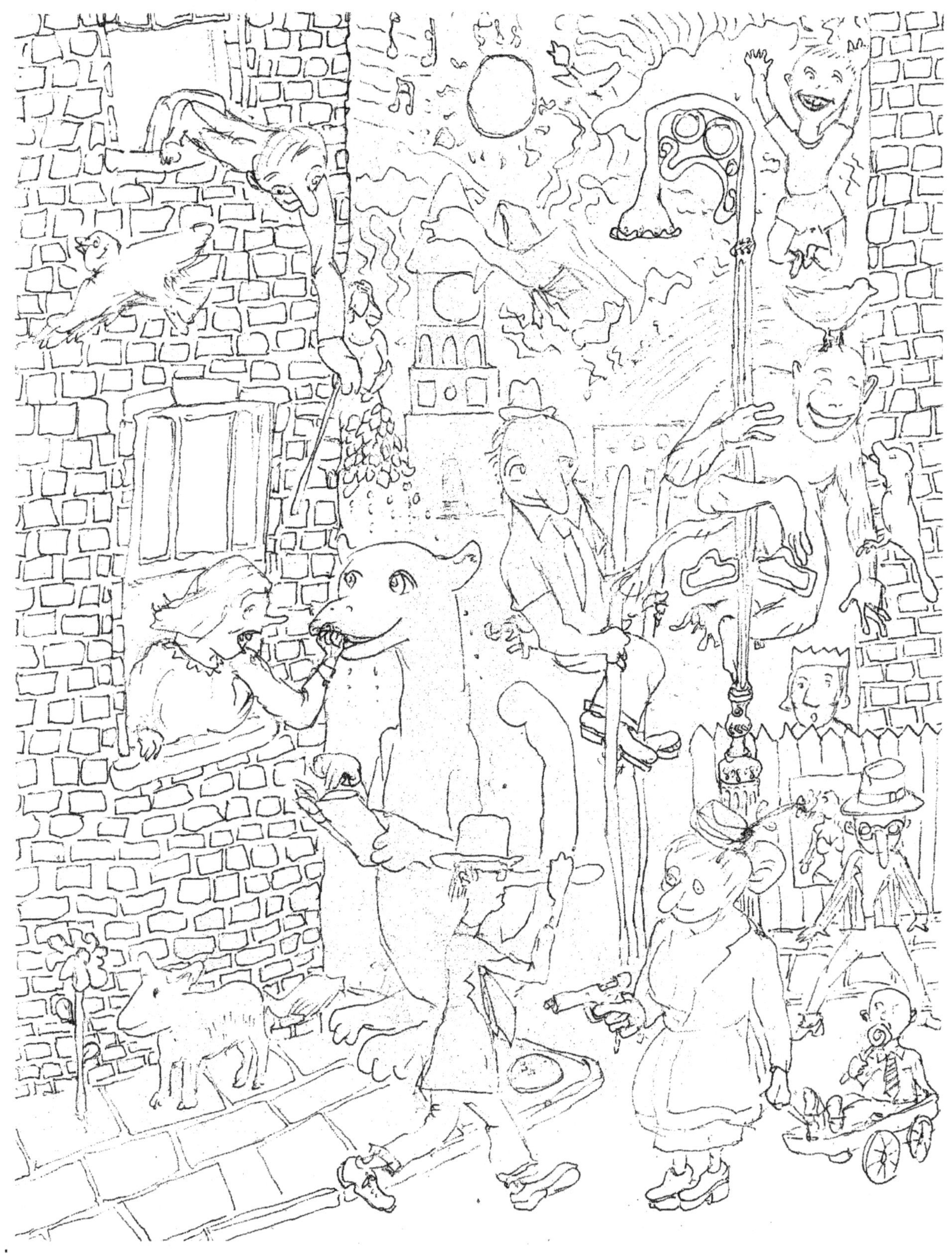

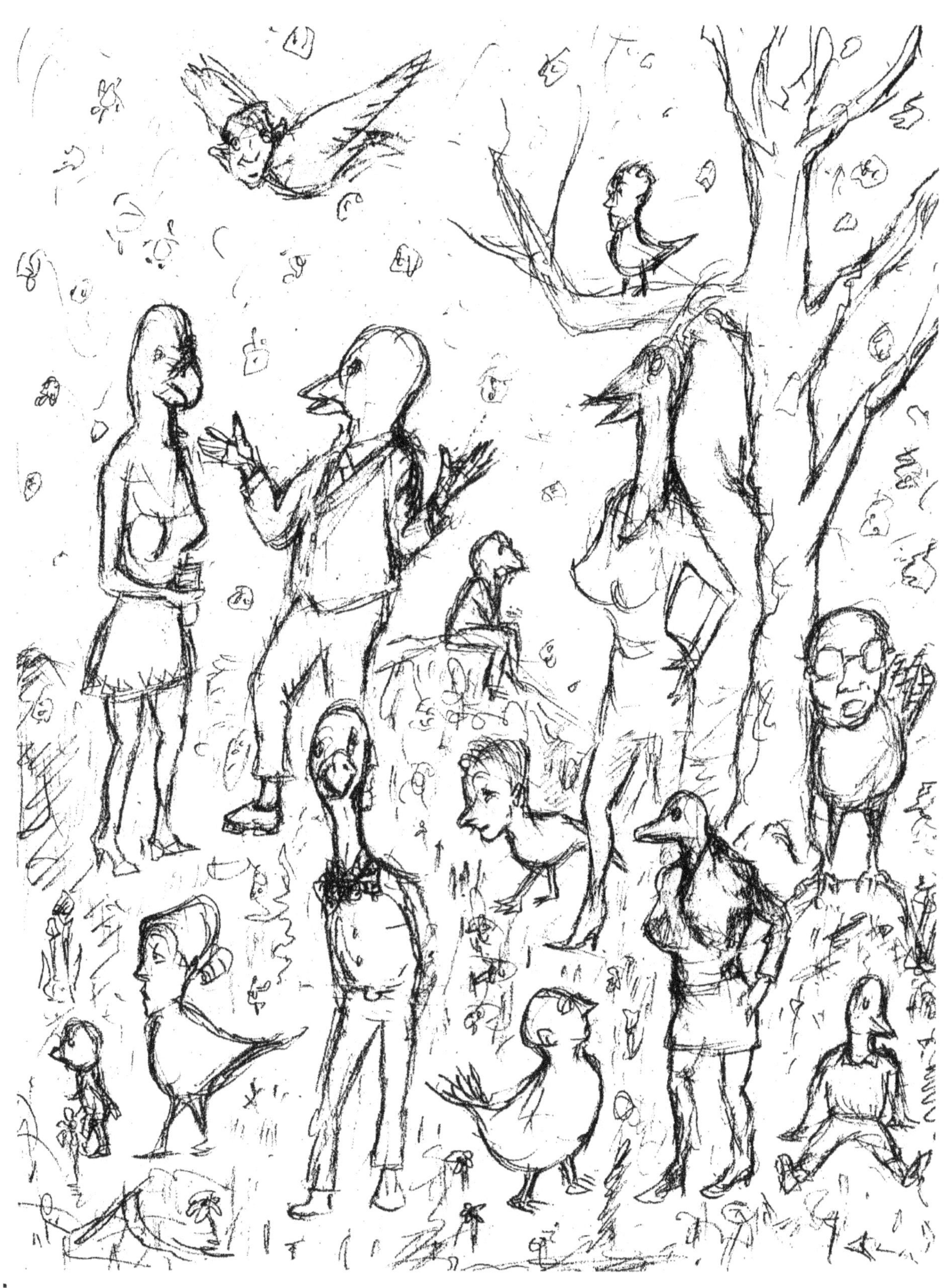

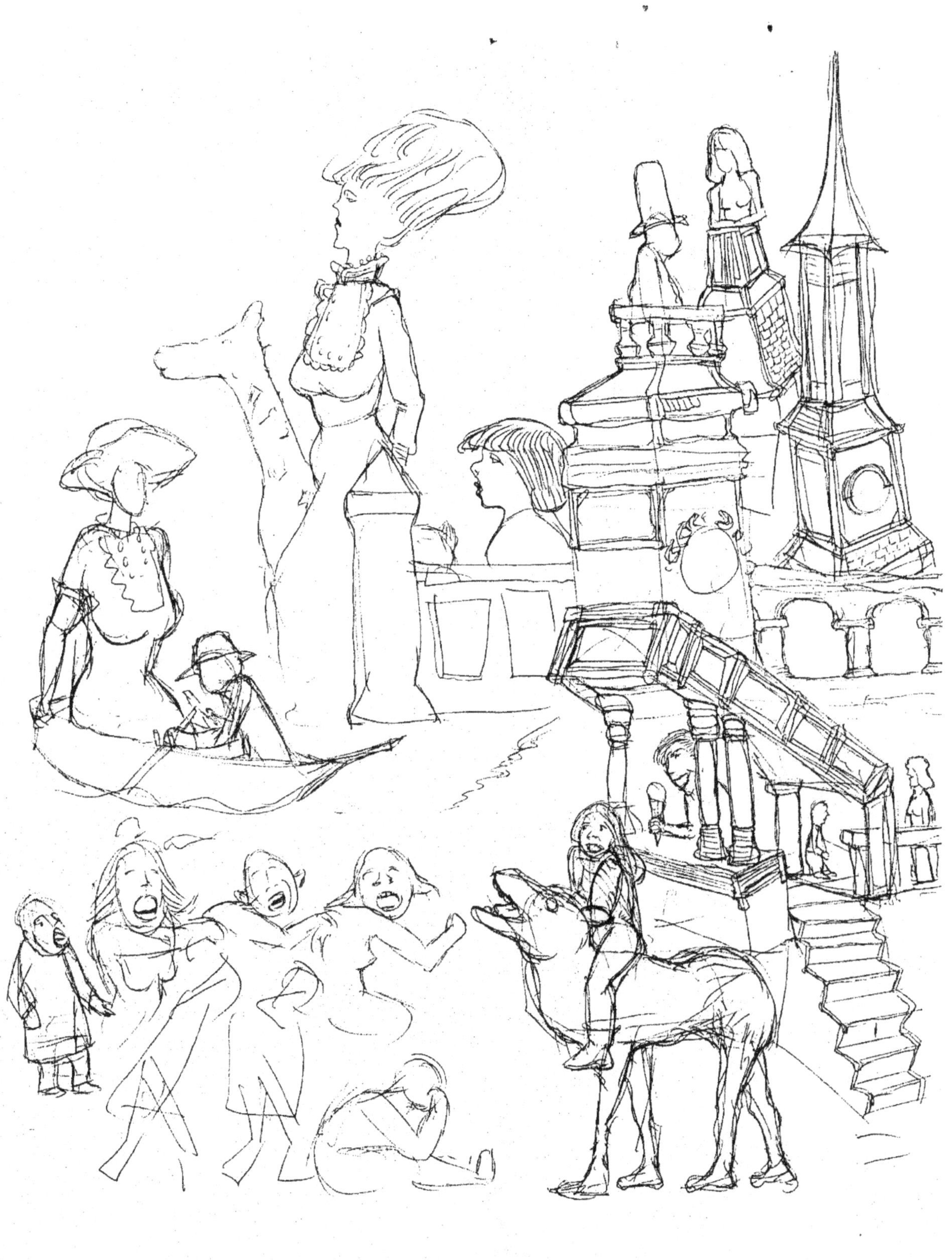

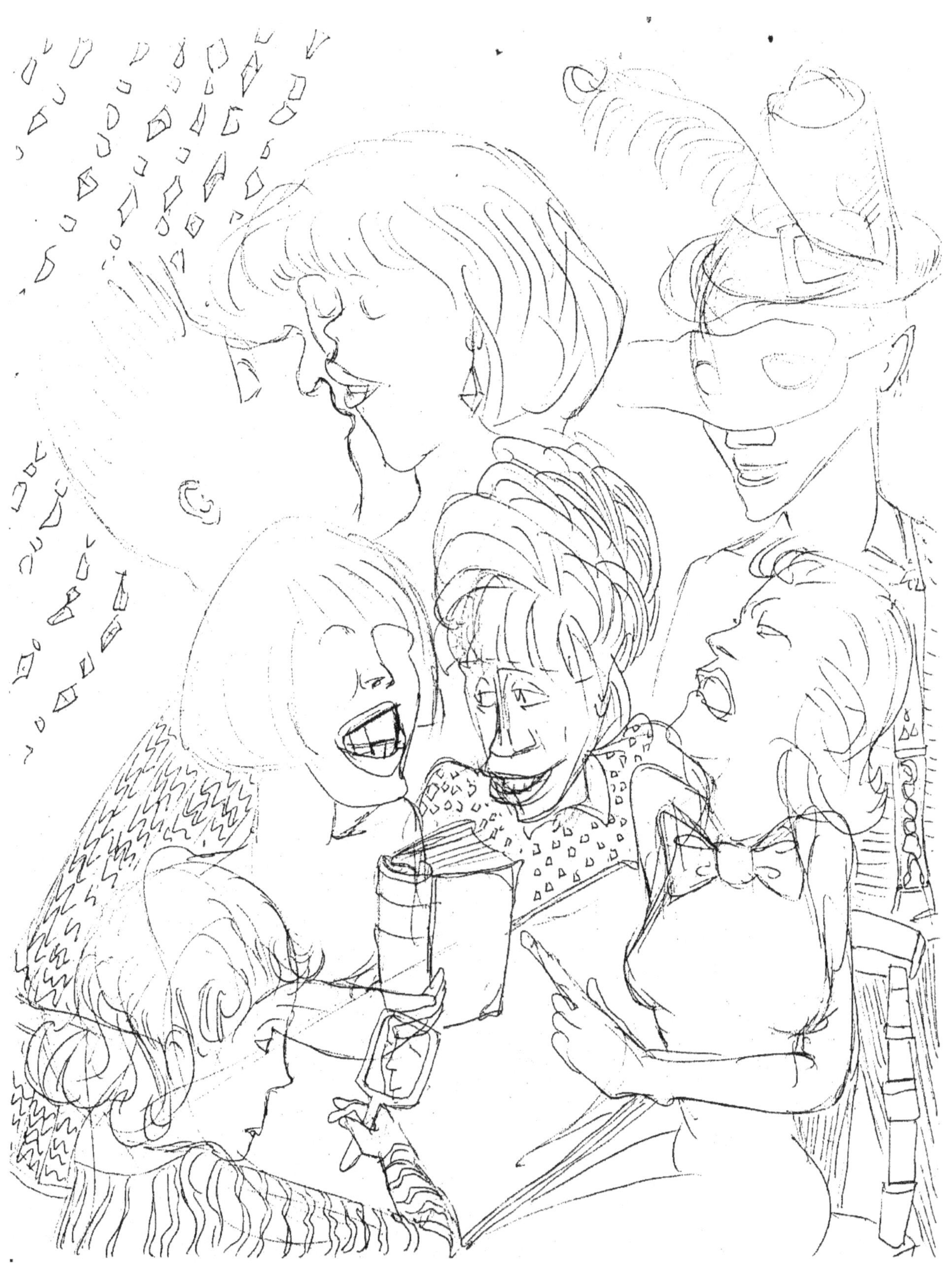

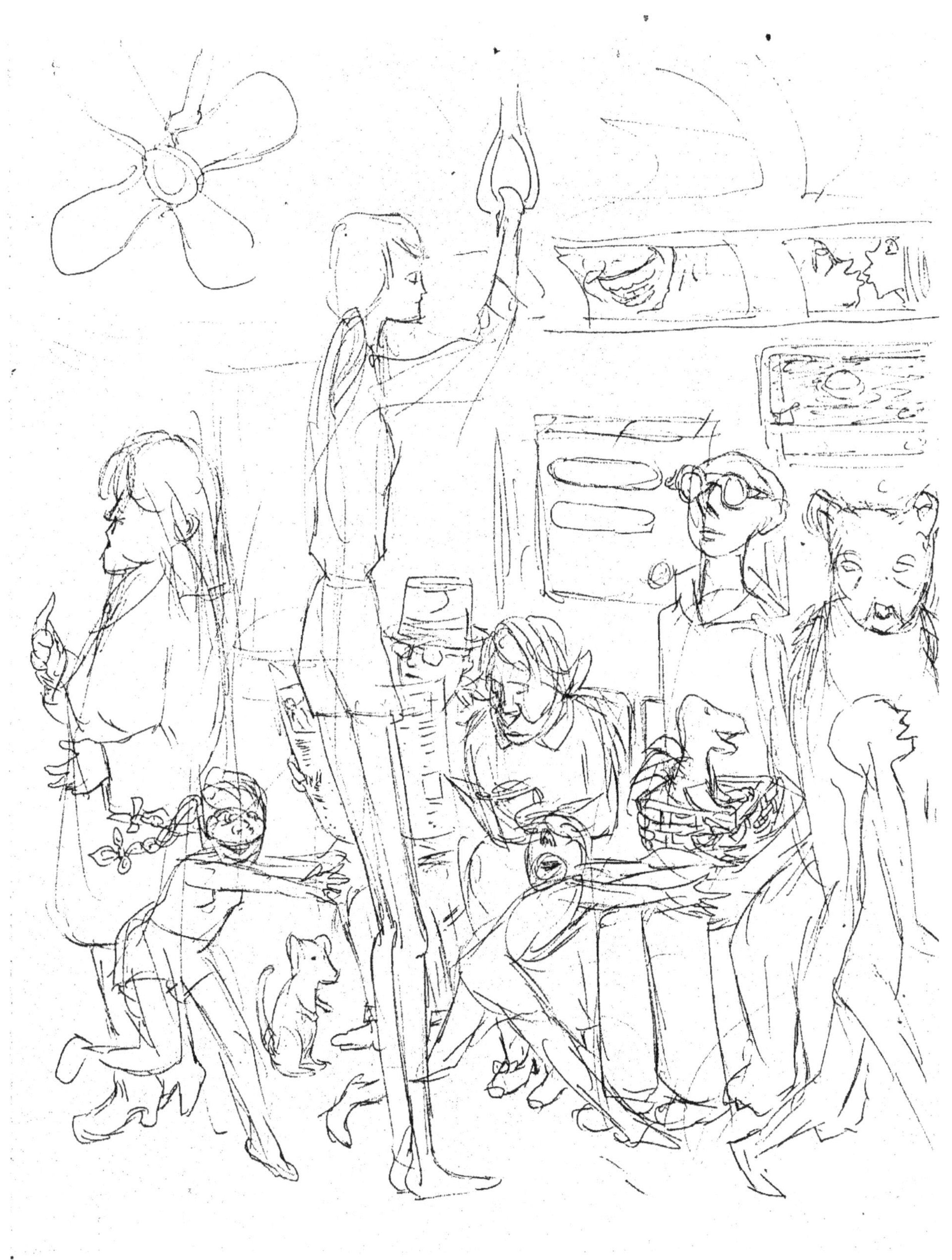

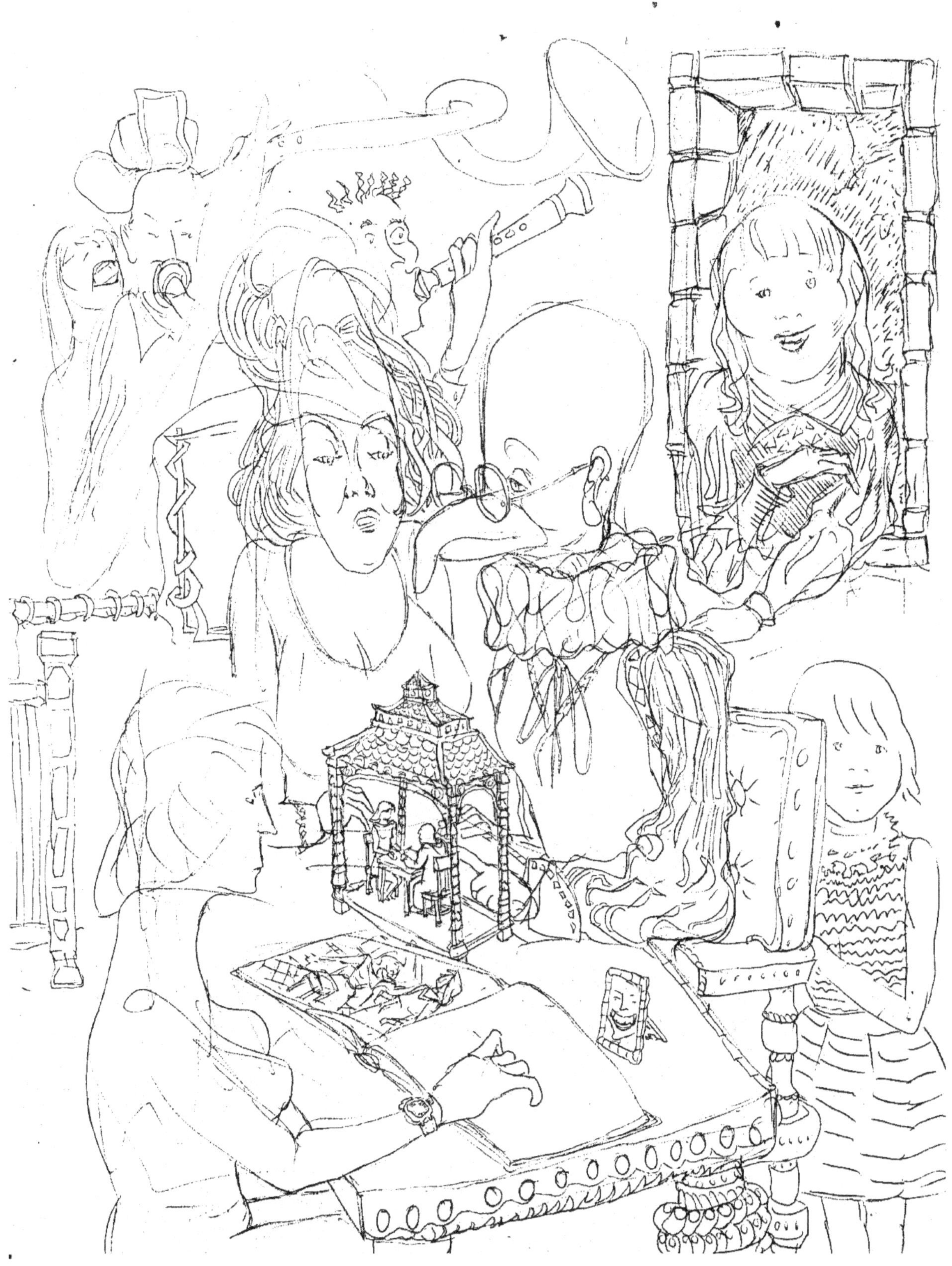

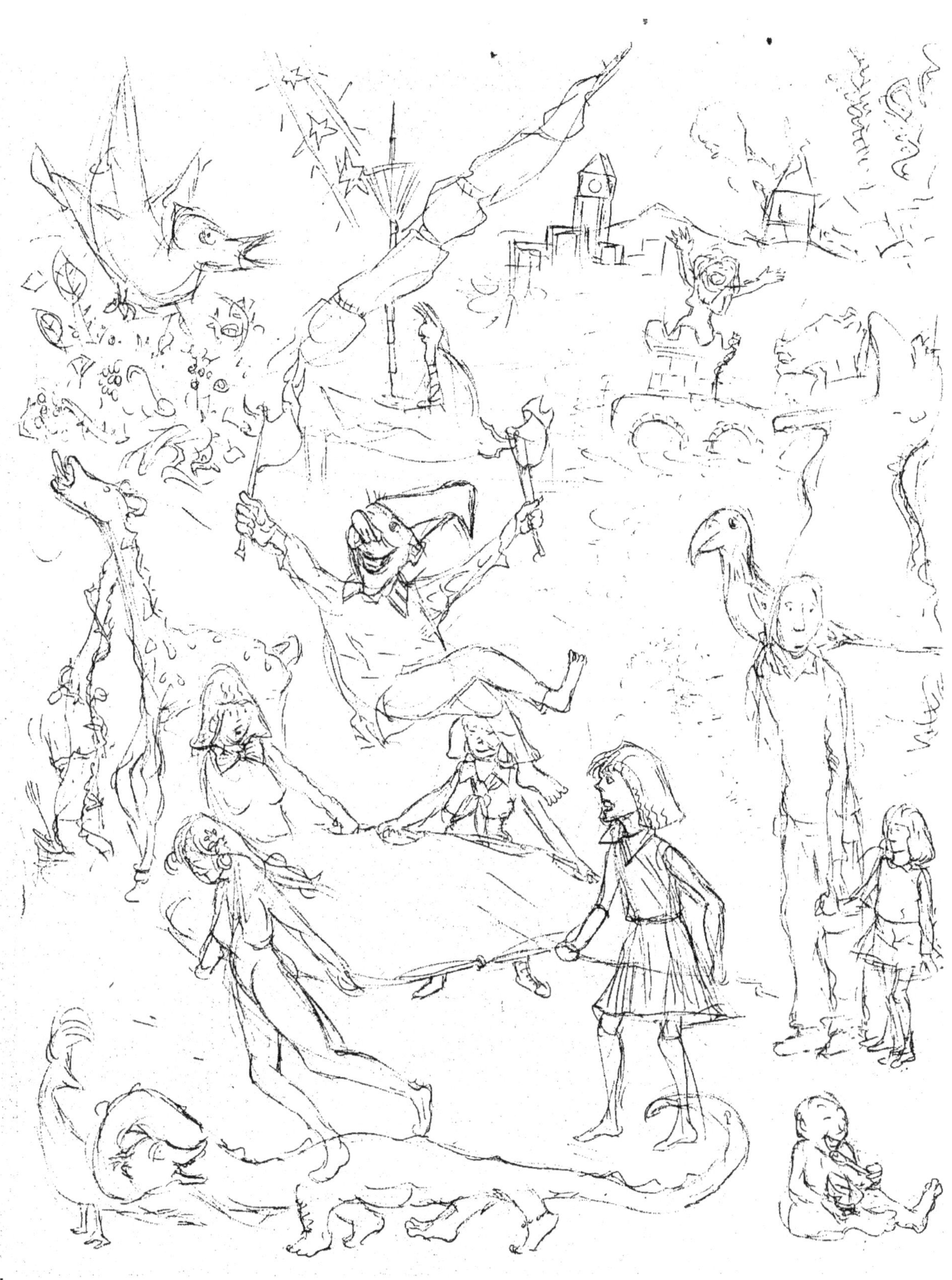

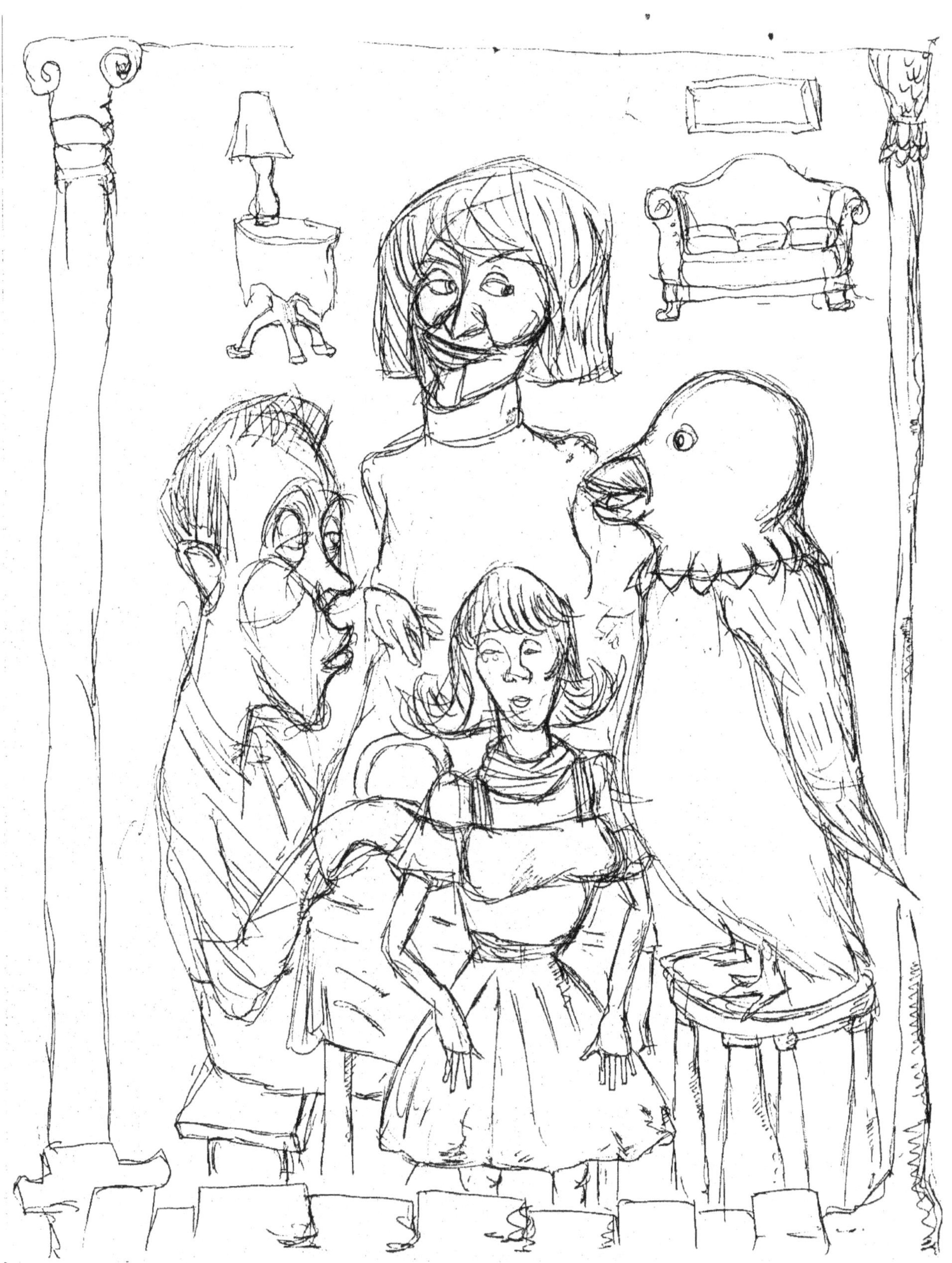

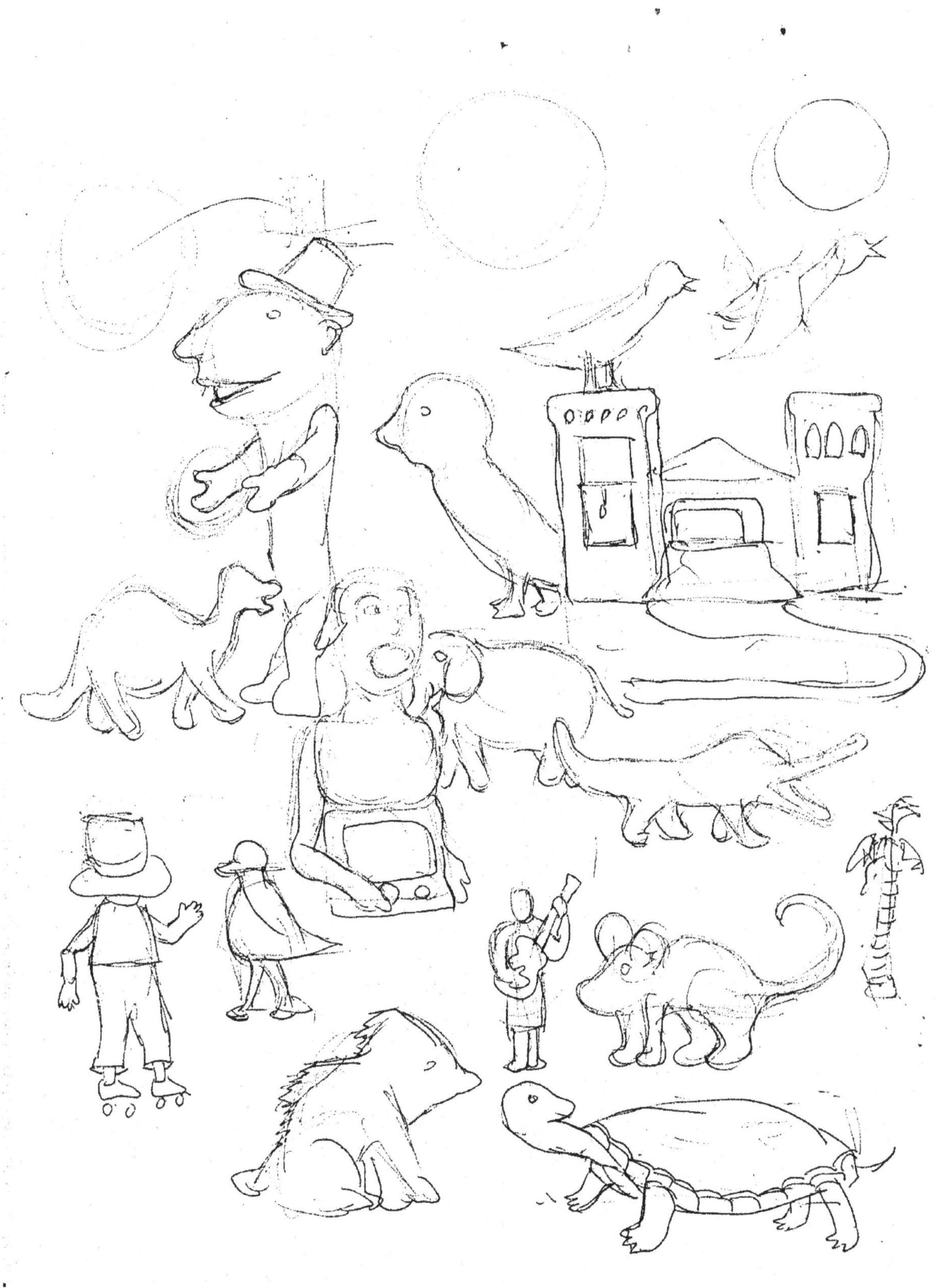

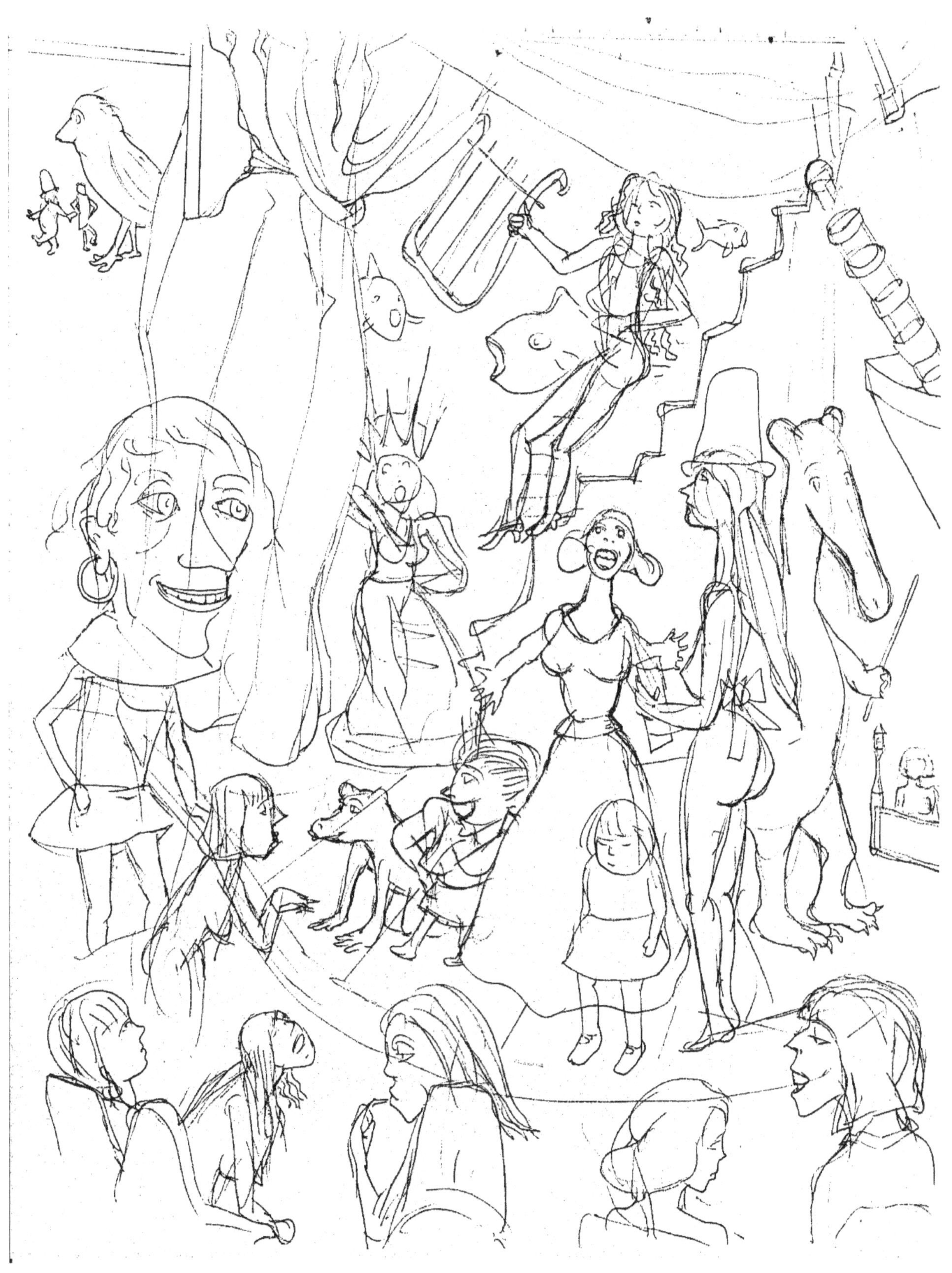

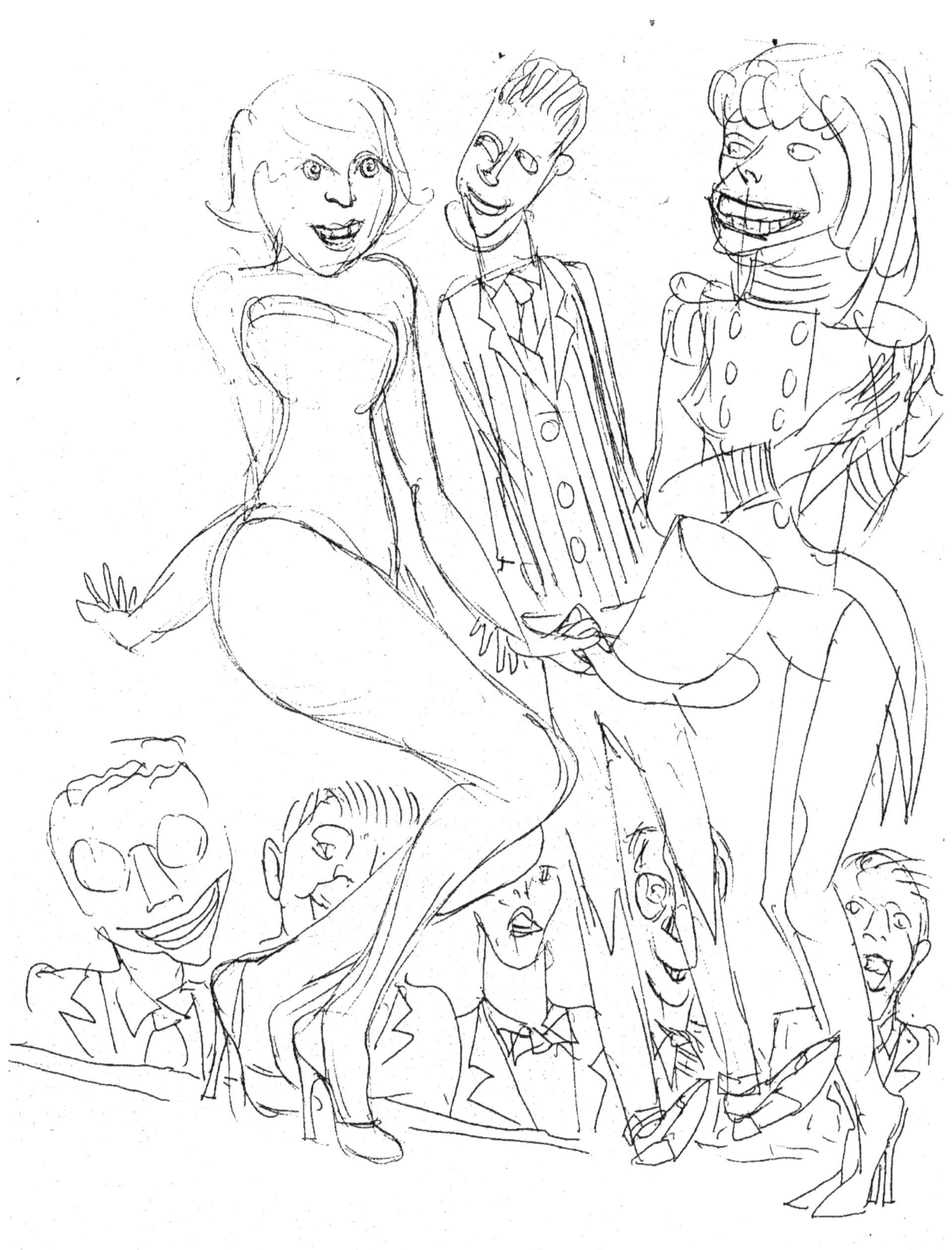

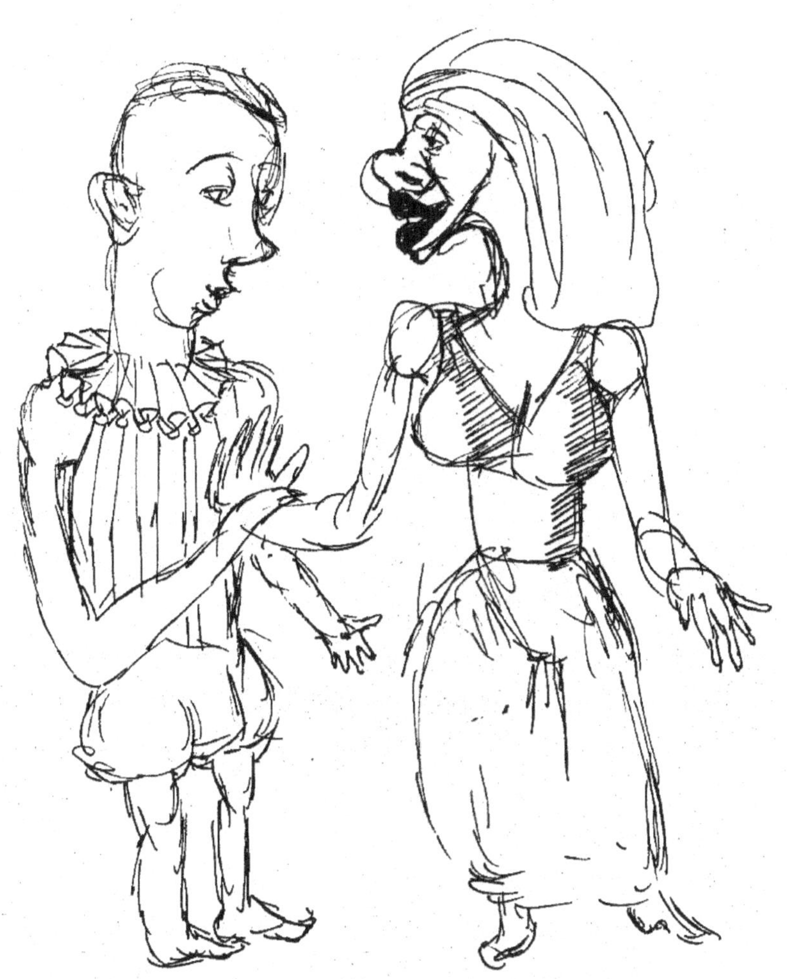

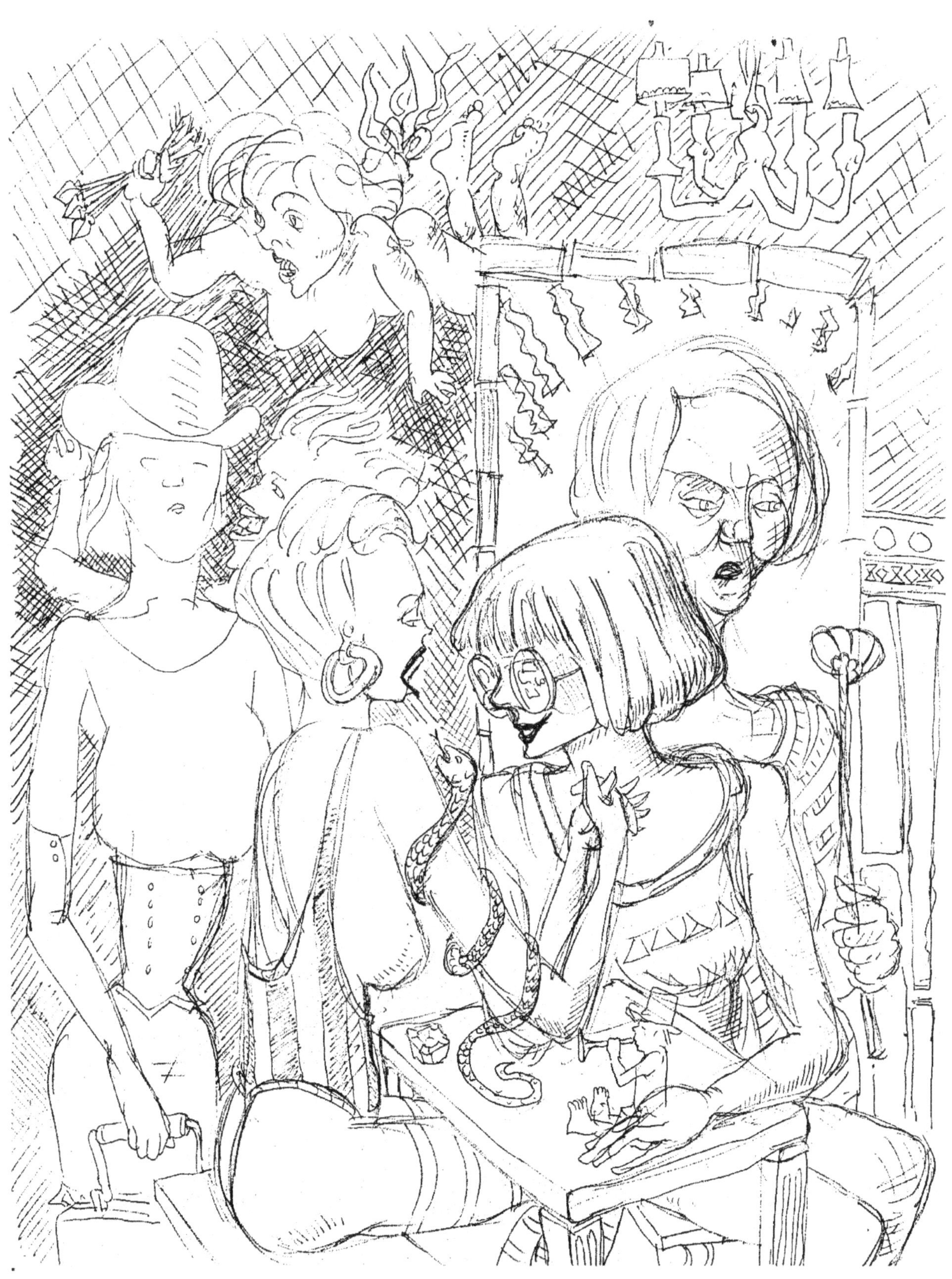

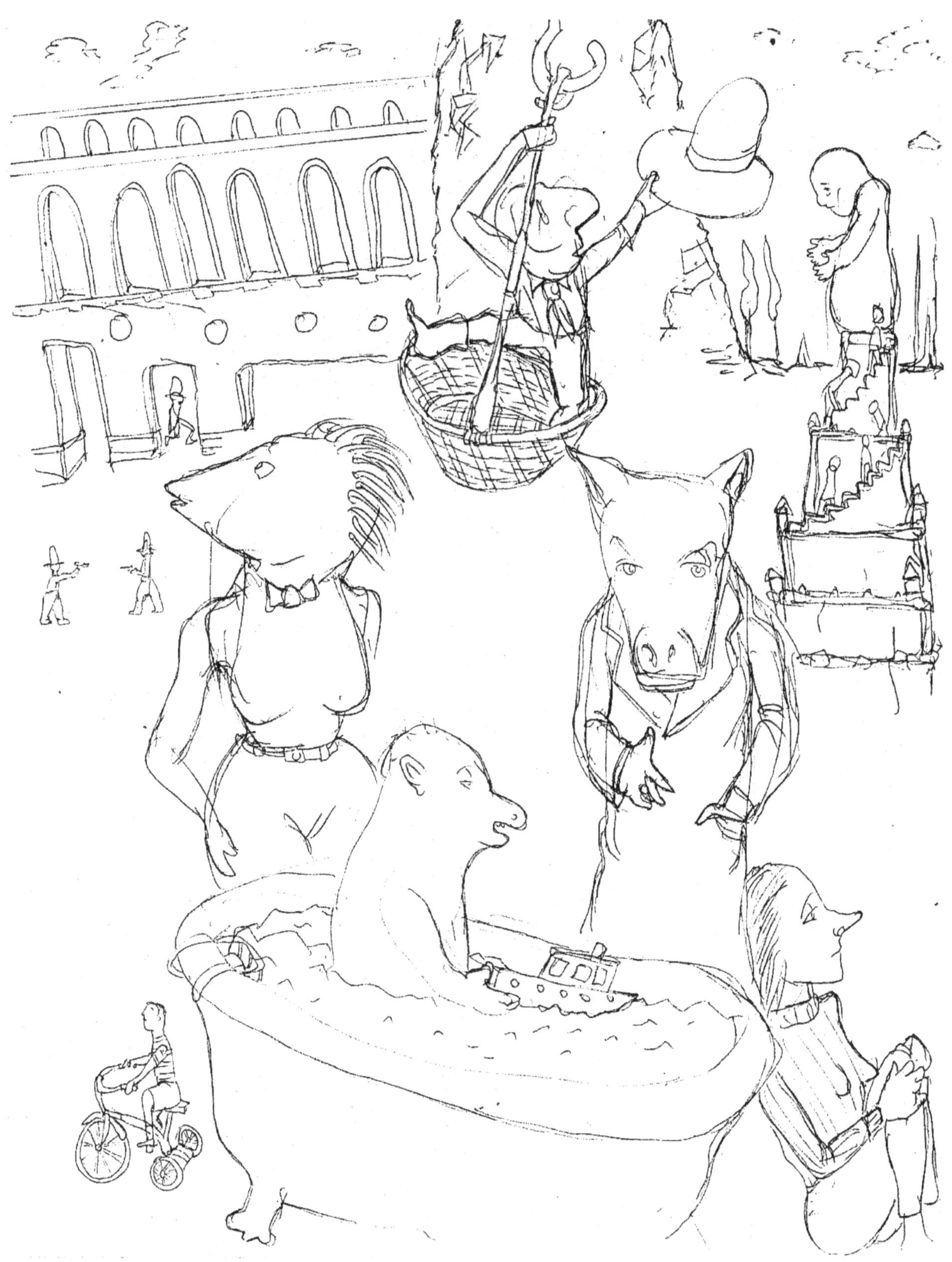

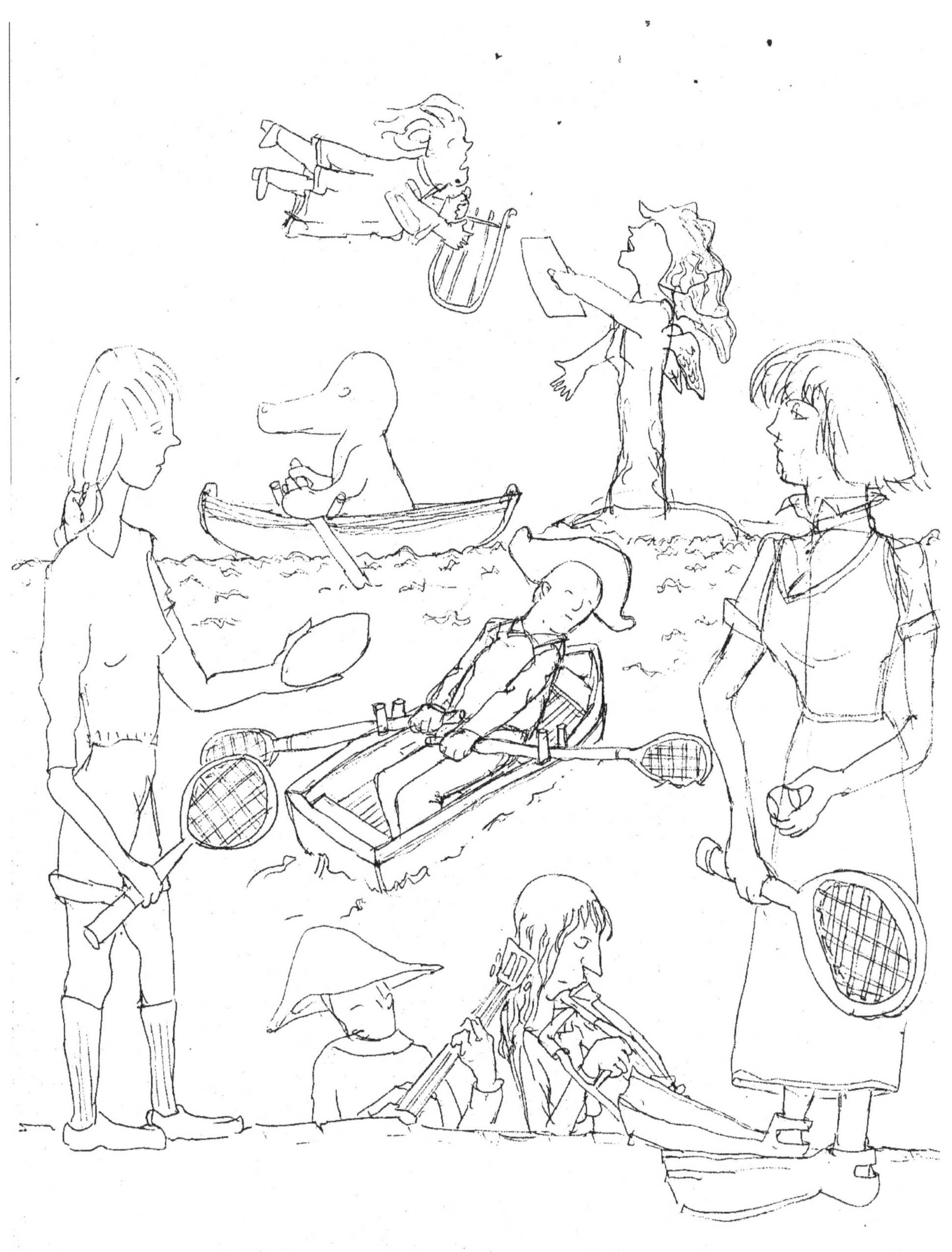

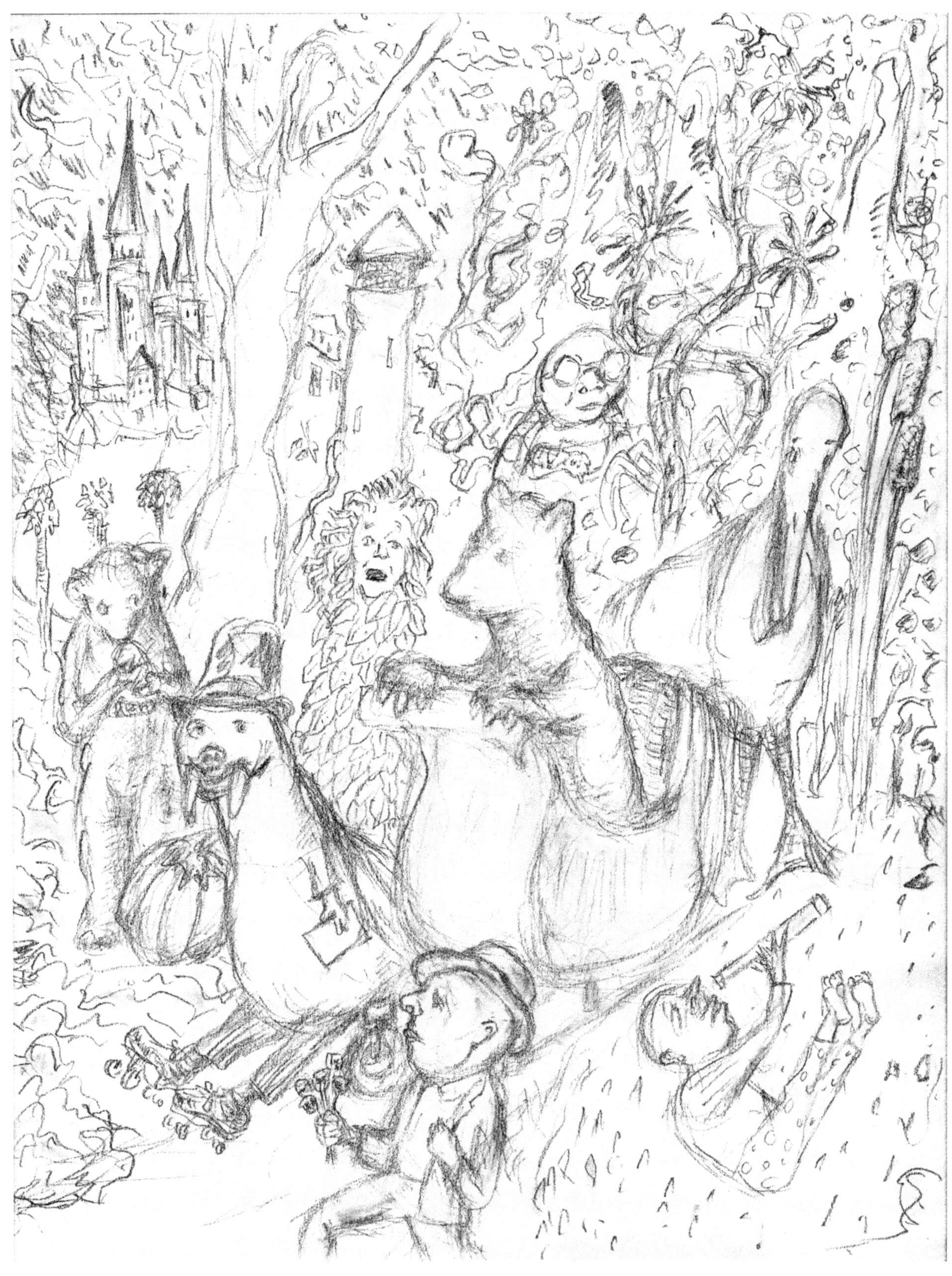

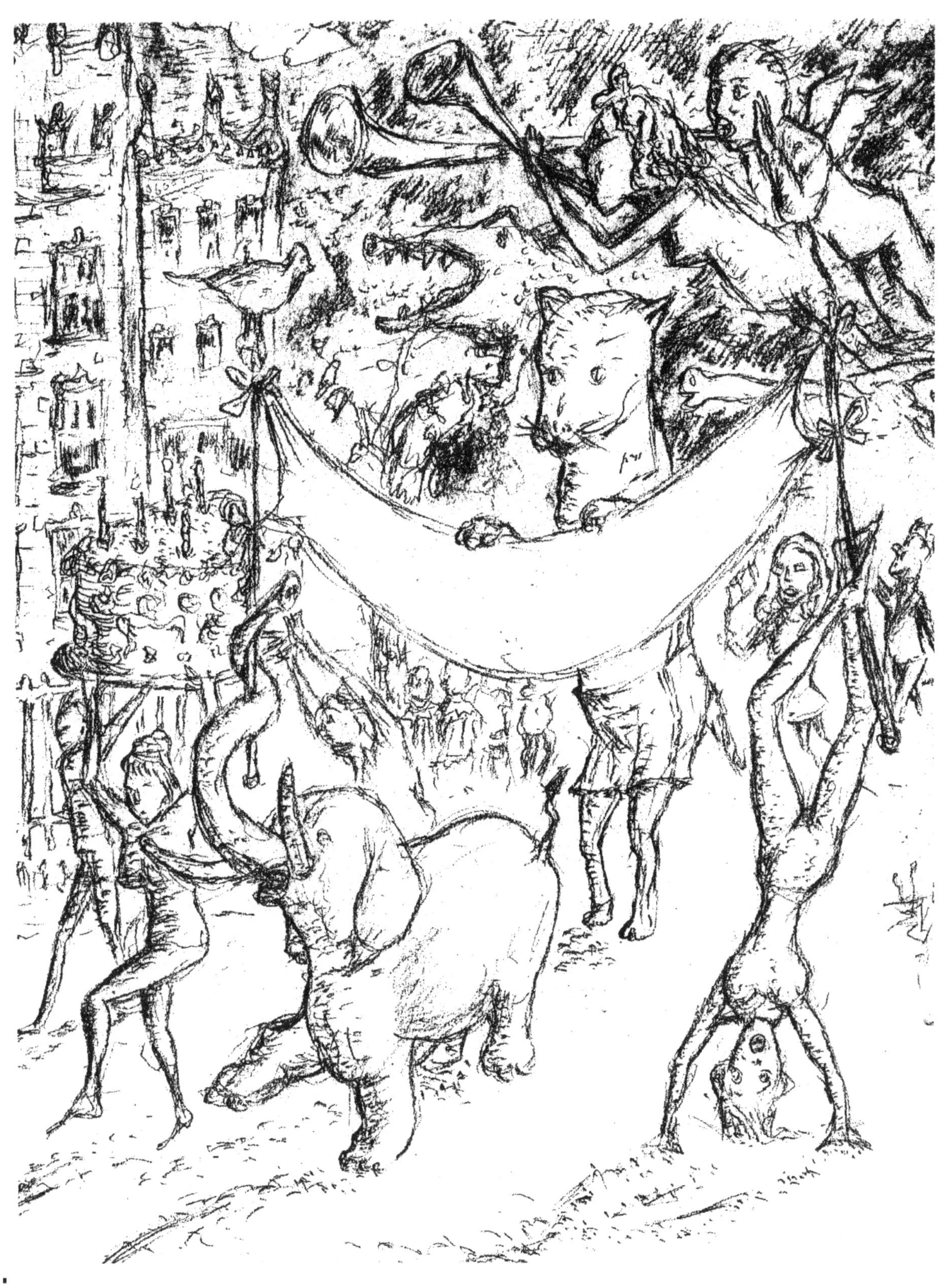

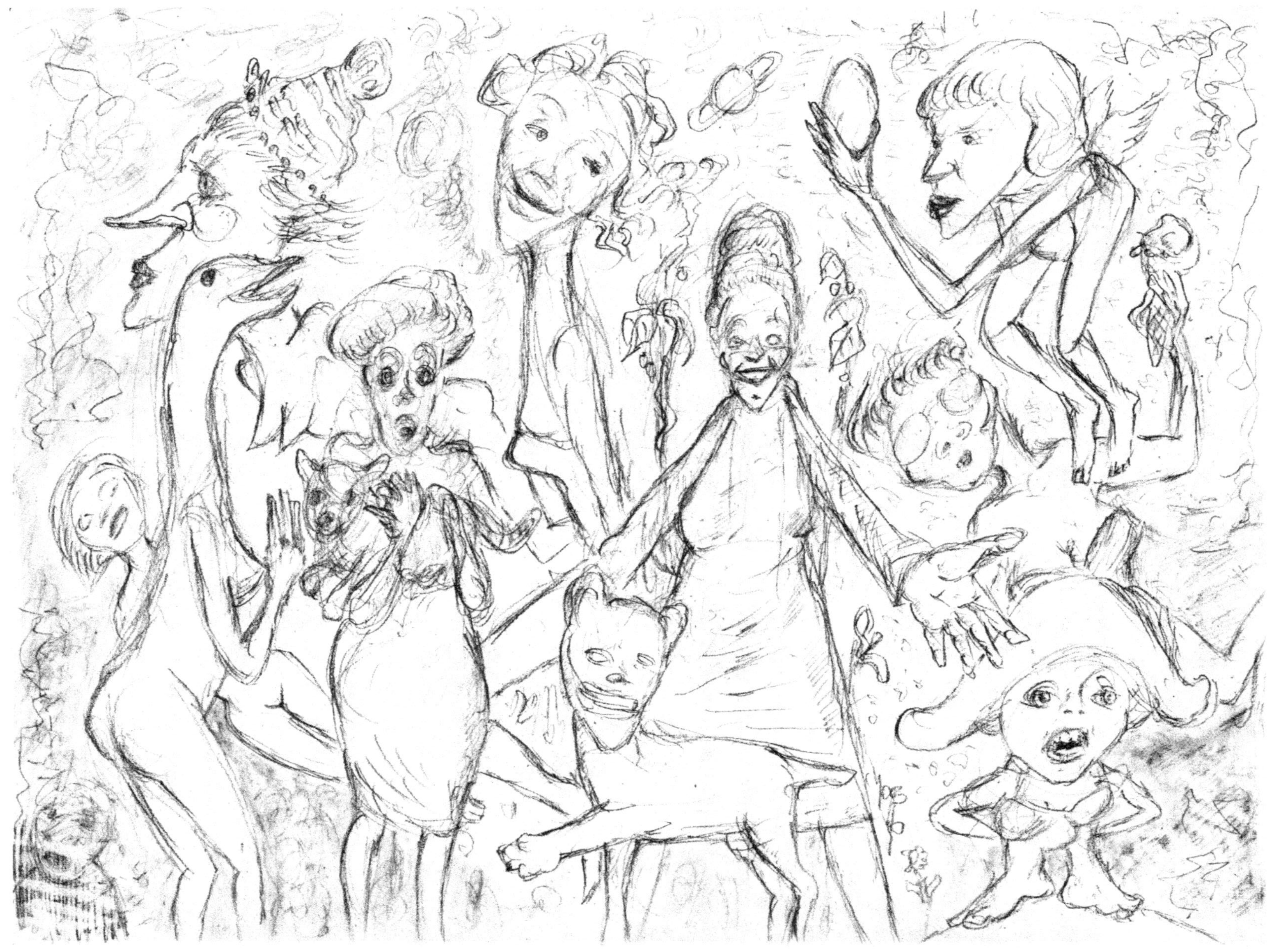

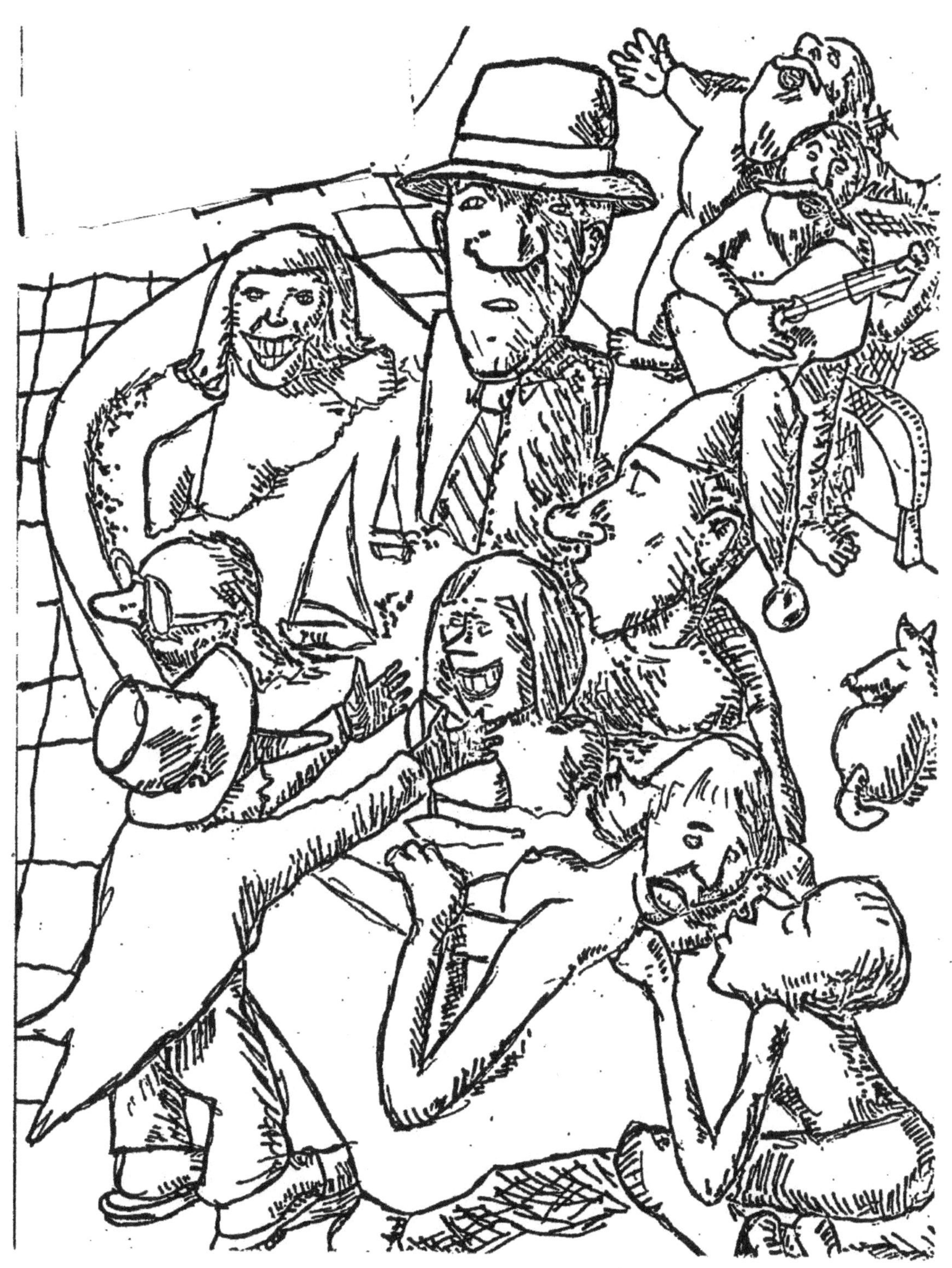

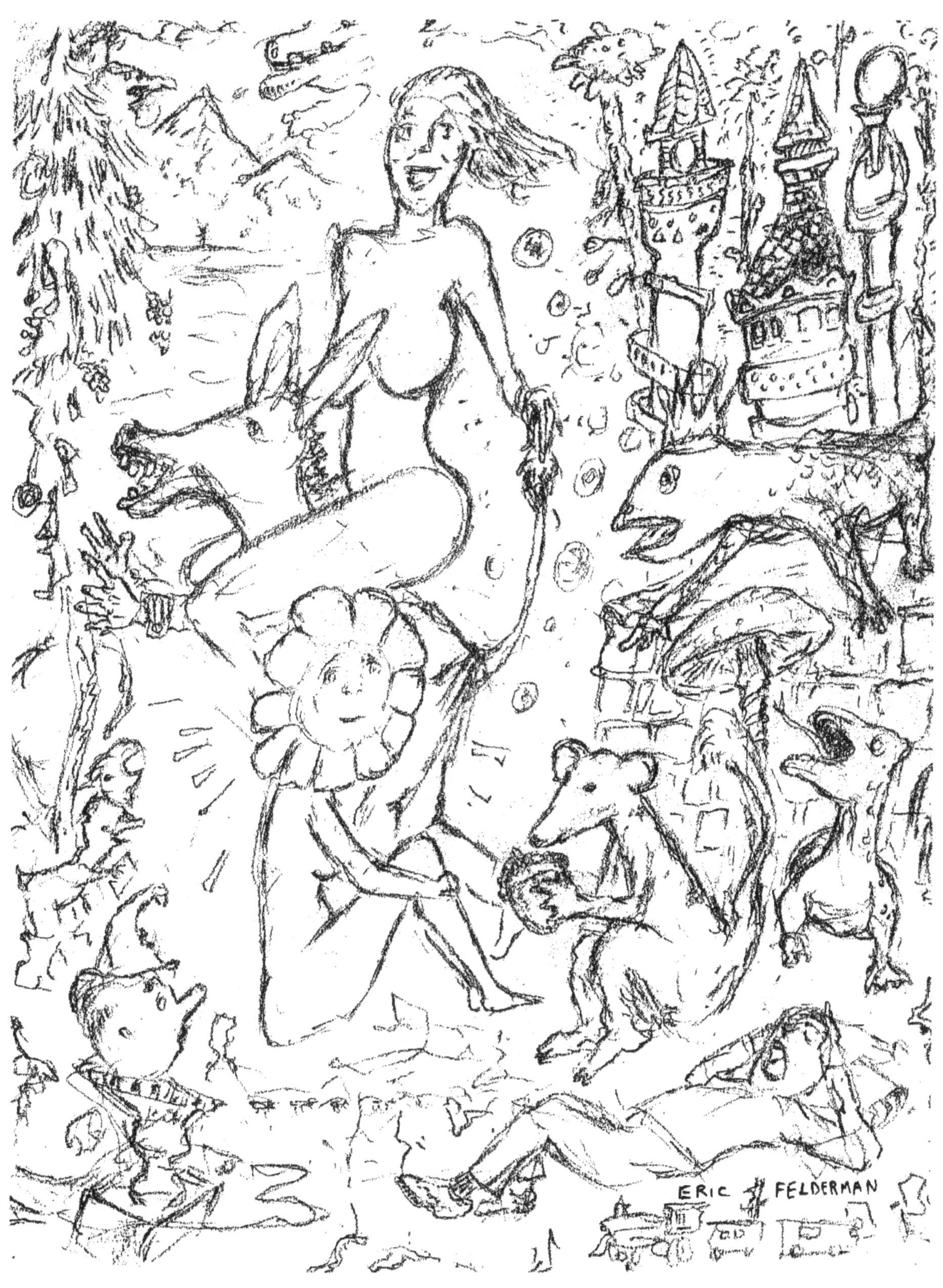

ERIC FELDERMAN

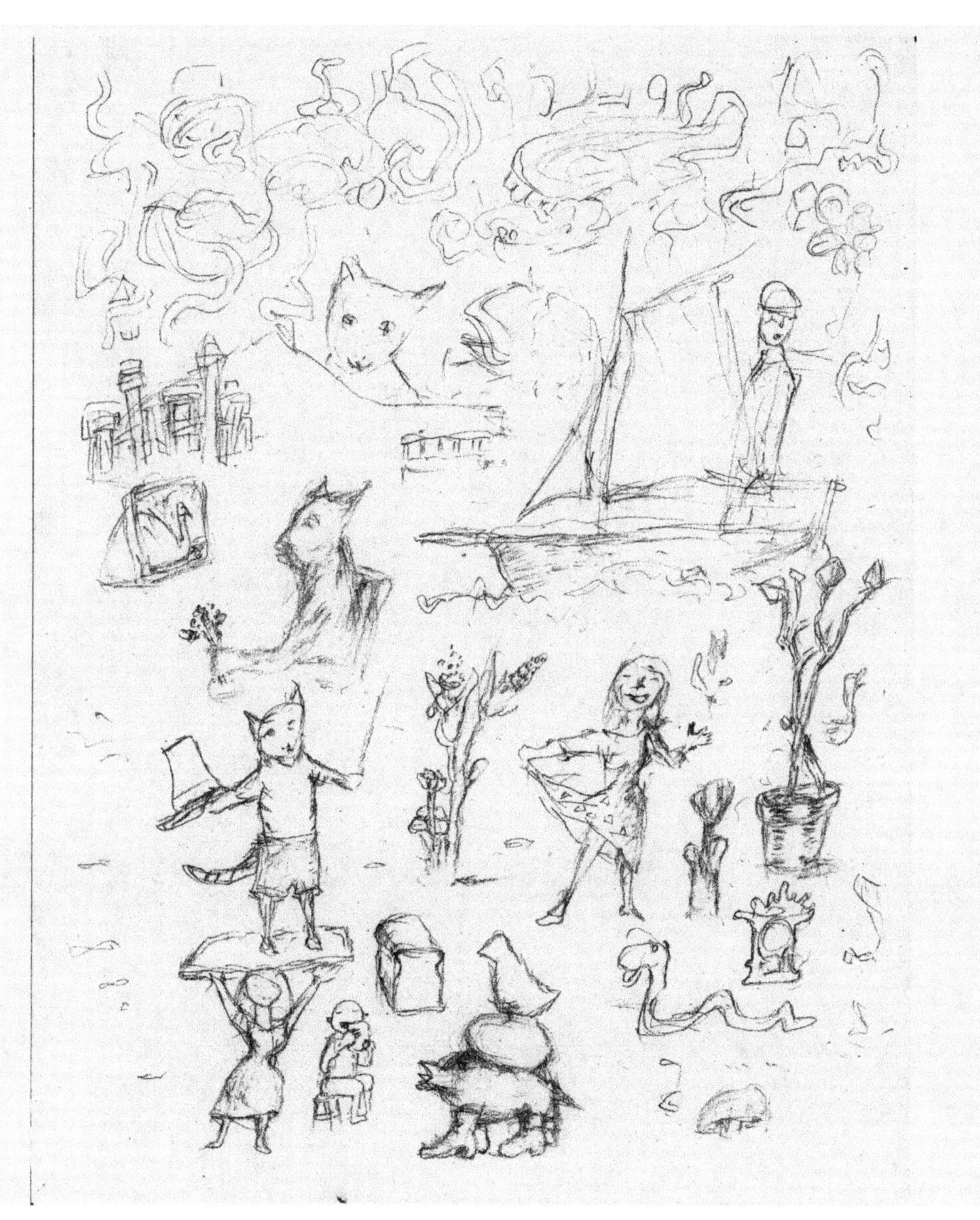

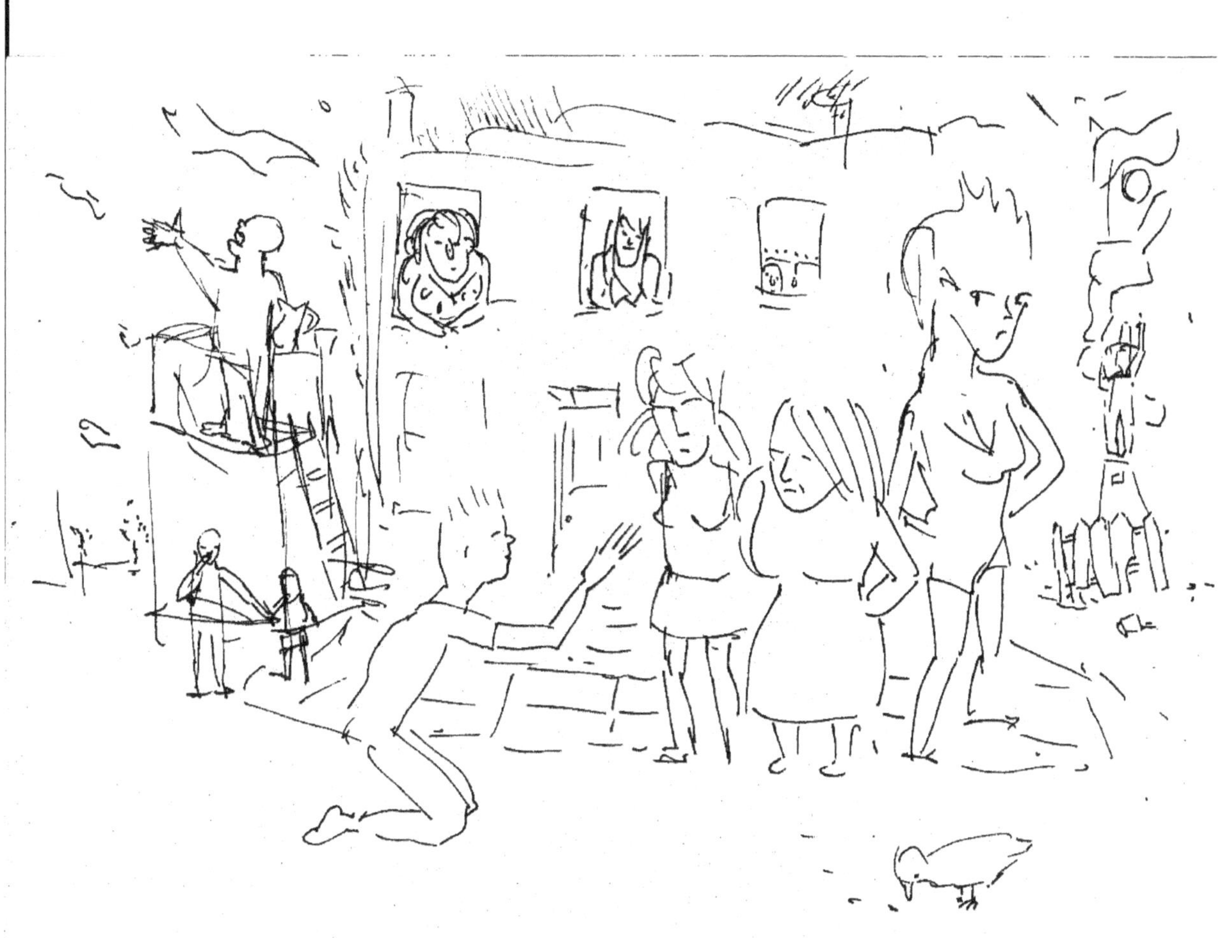

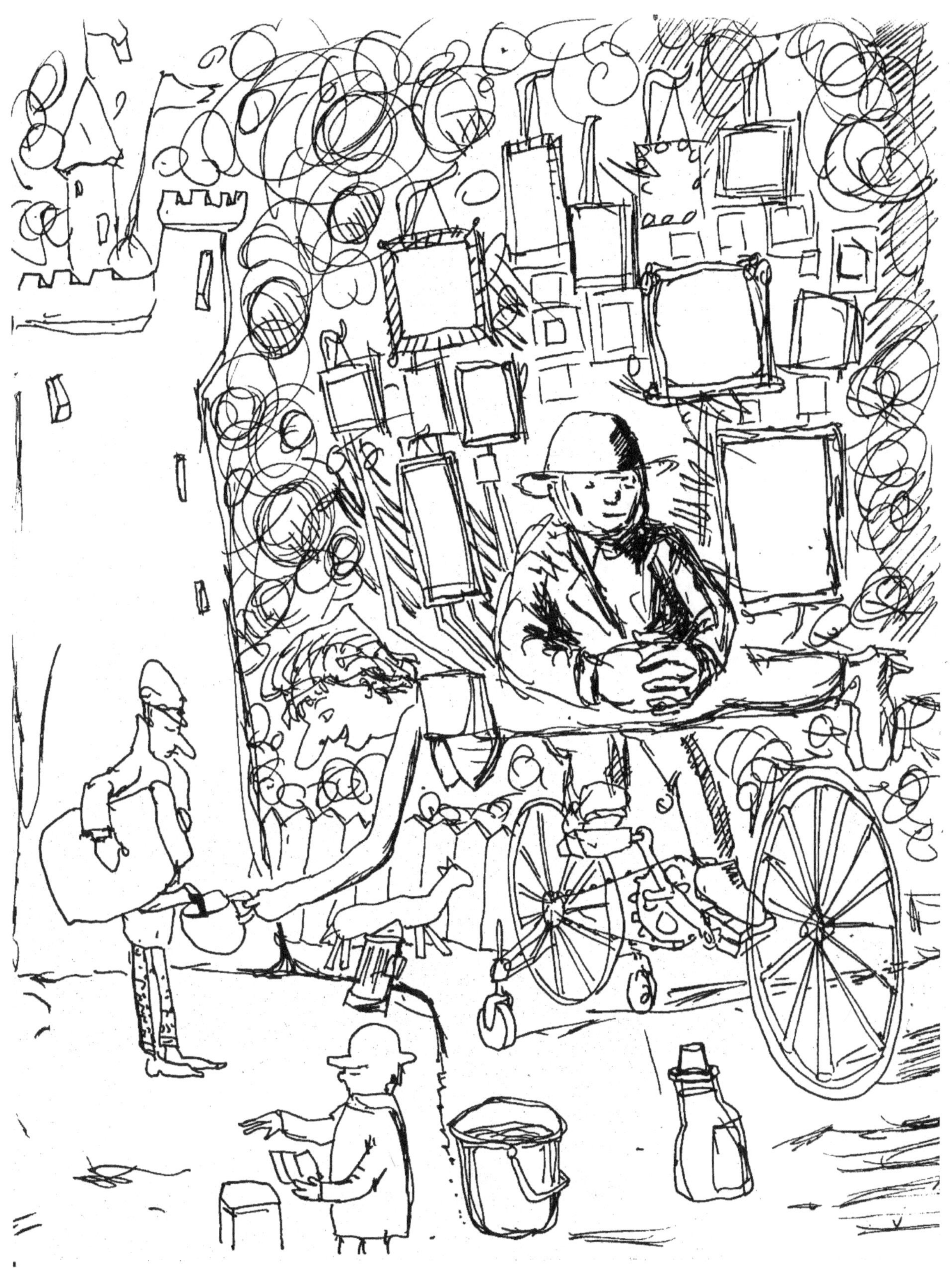

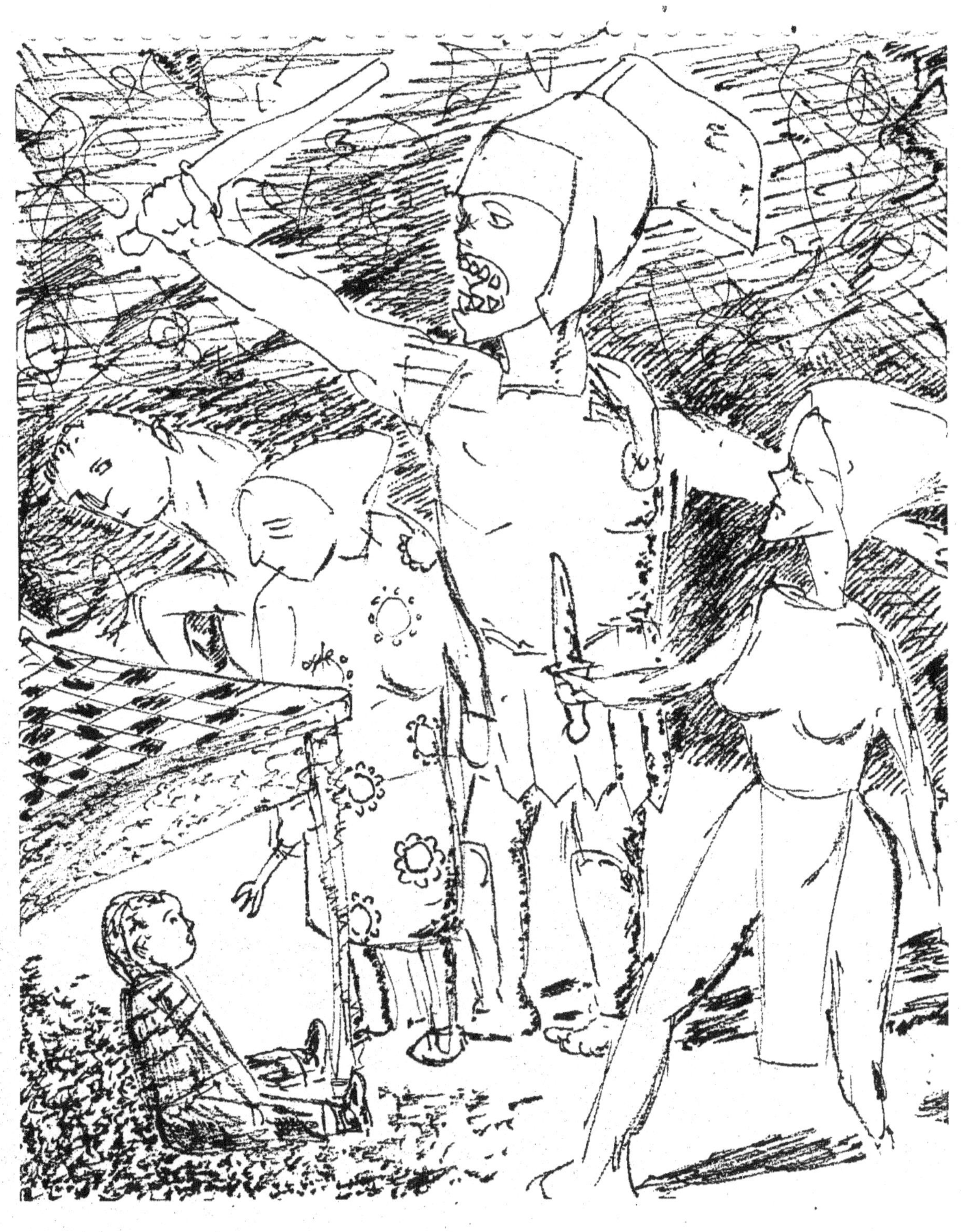

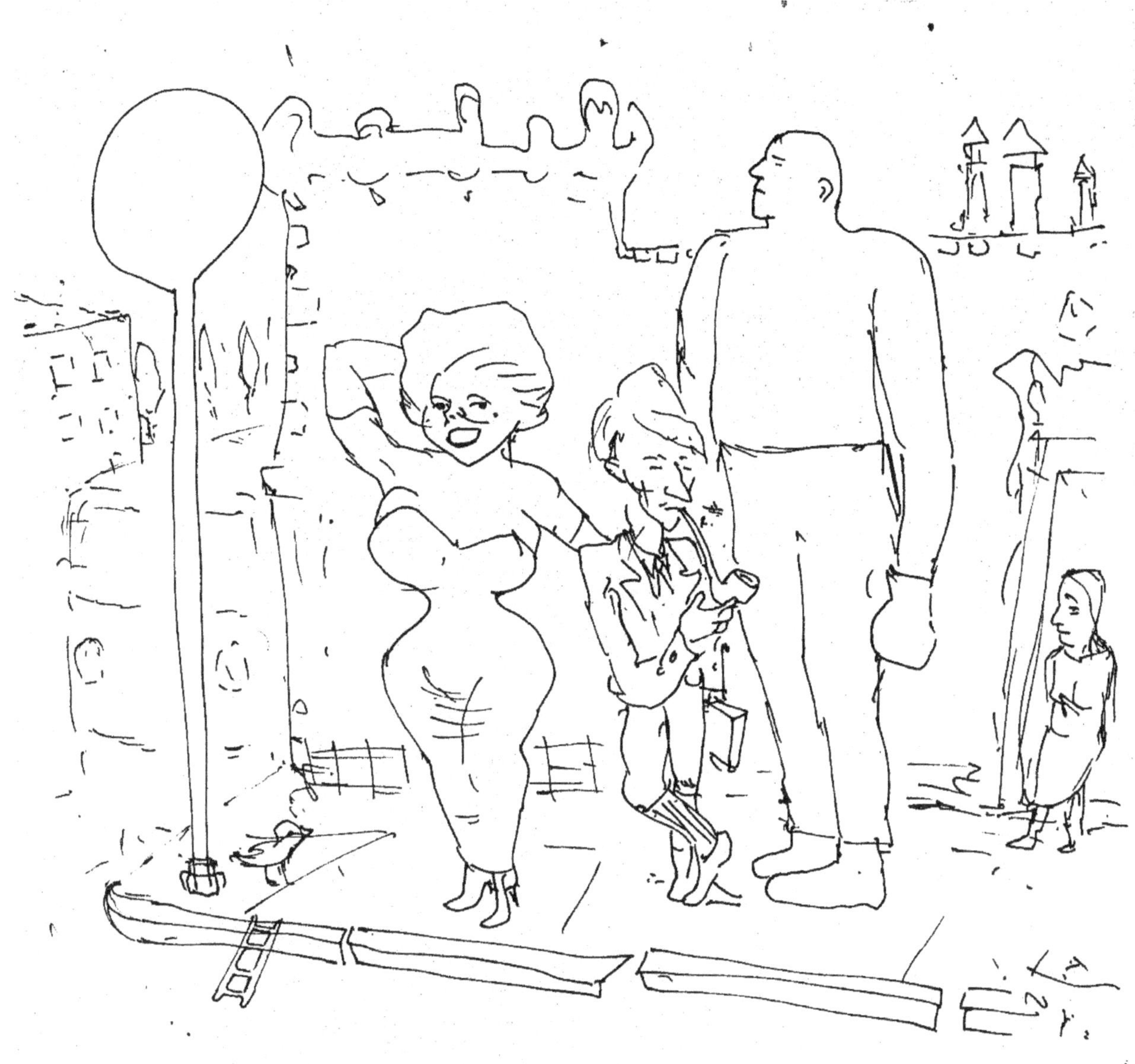

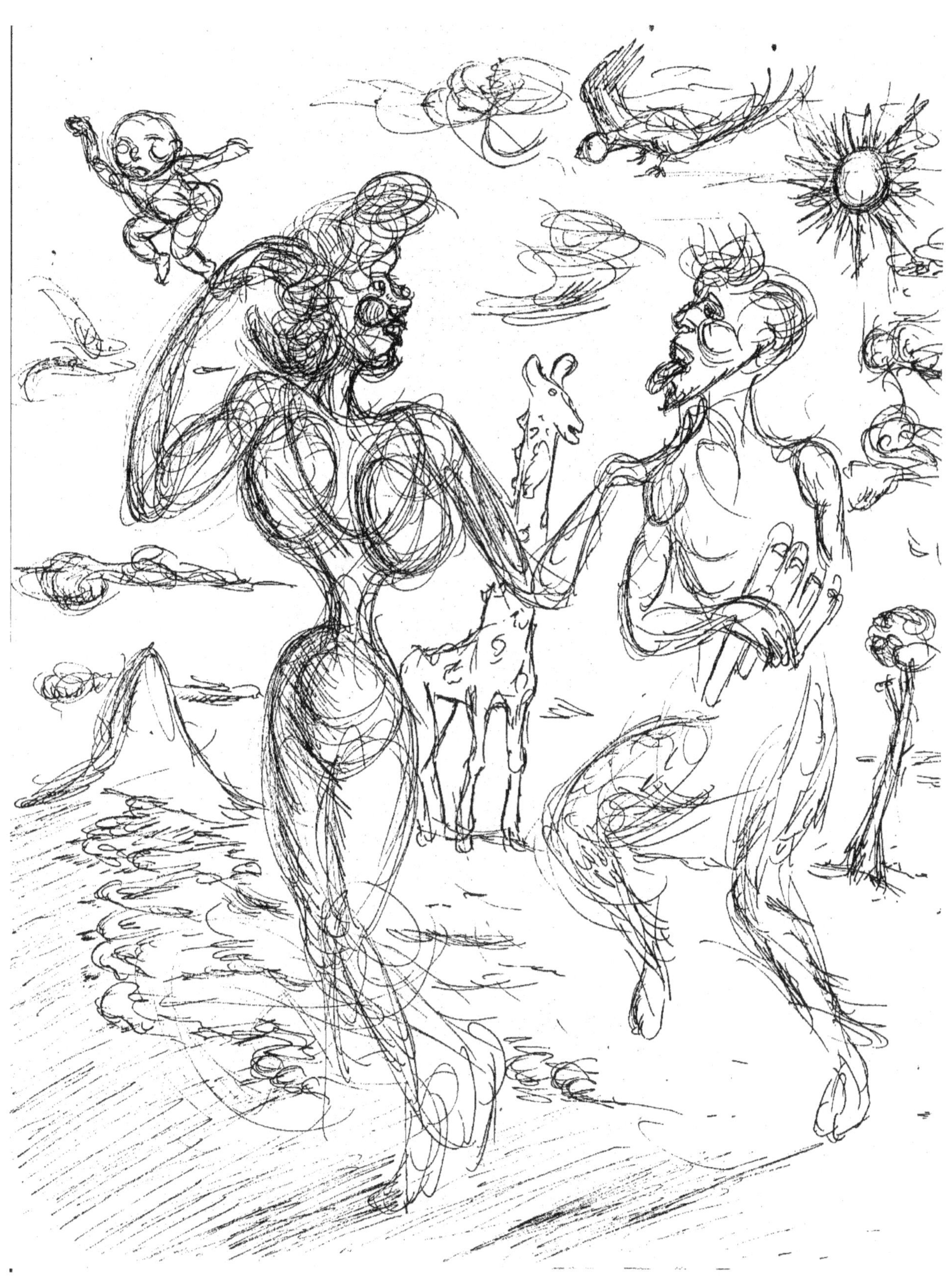

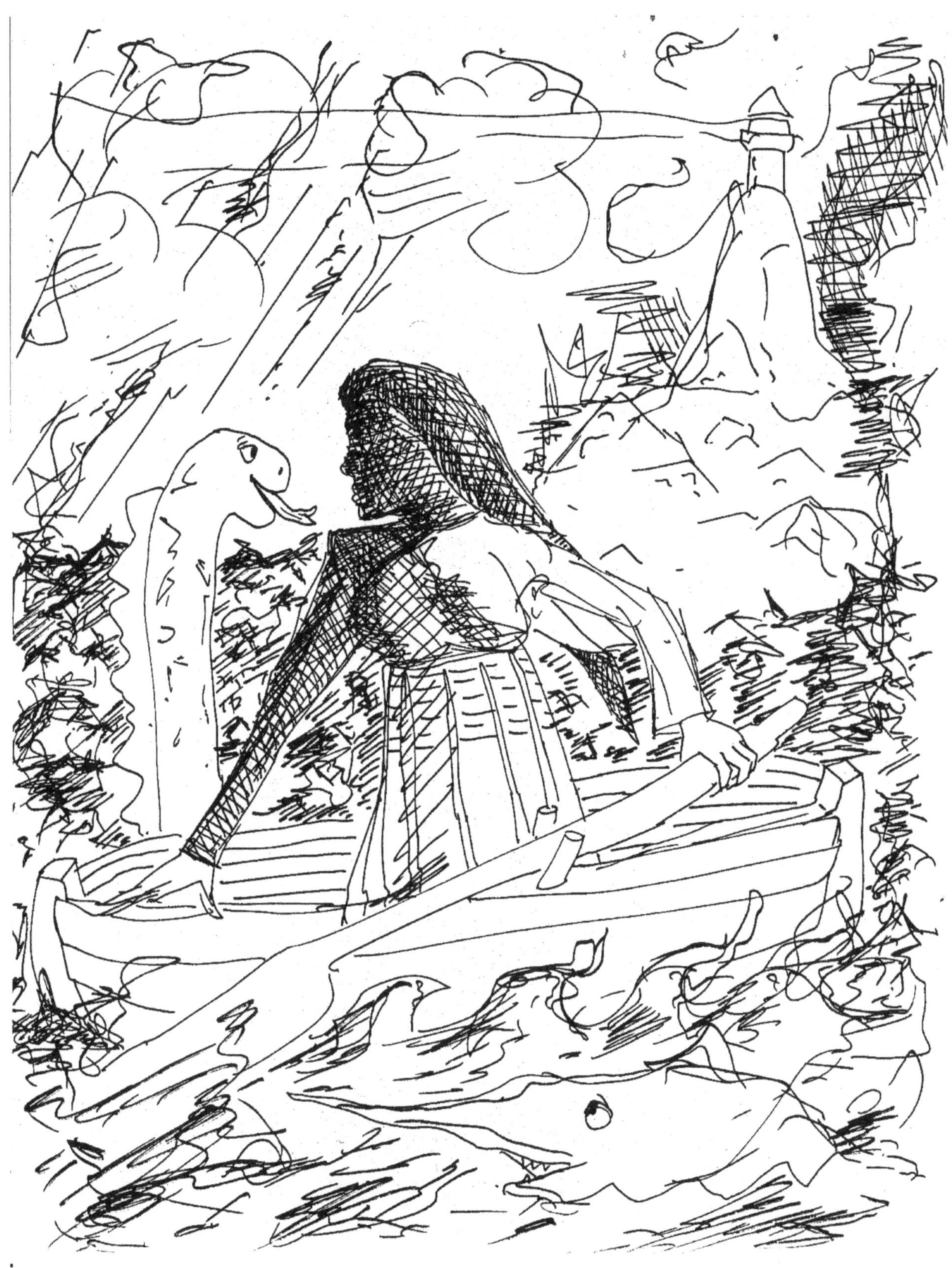

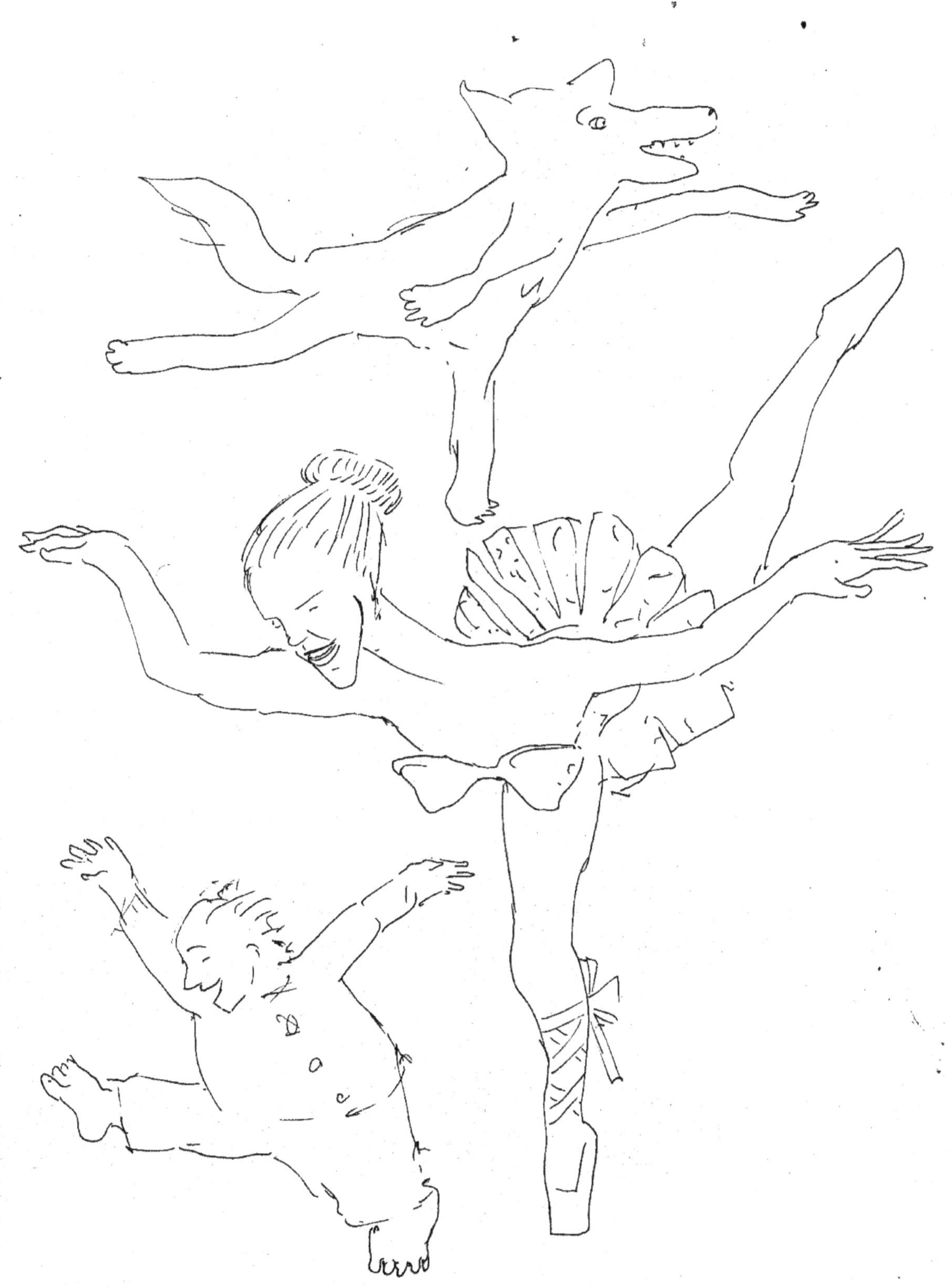

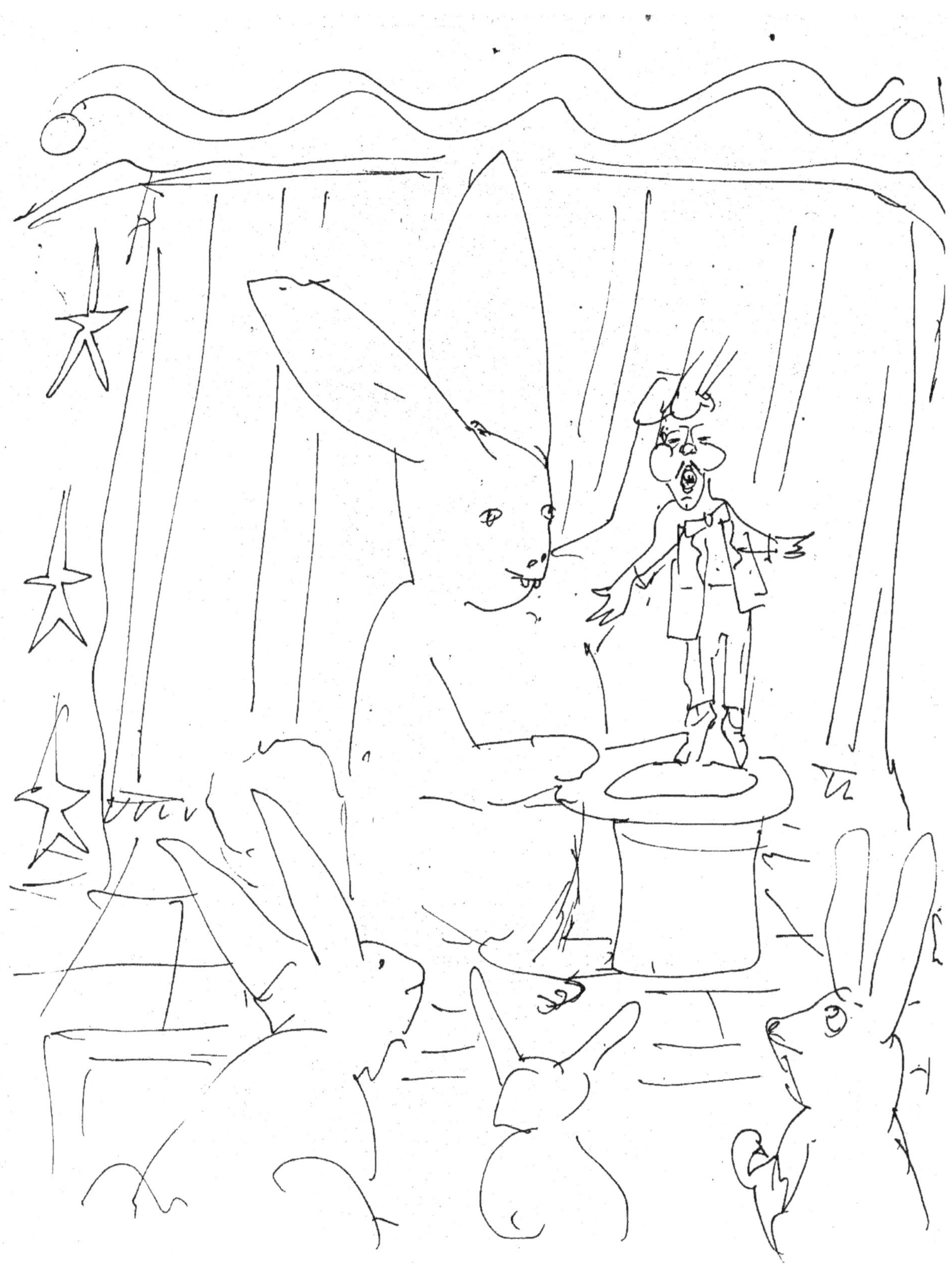

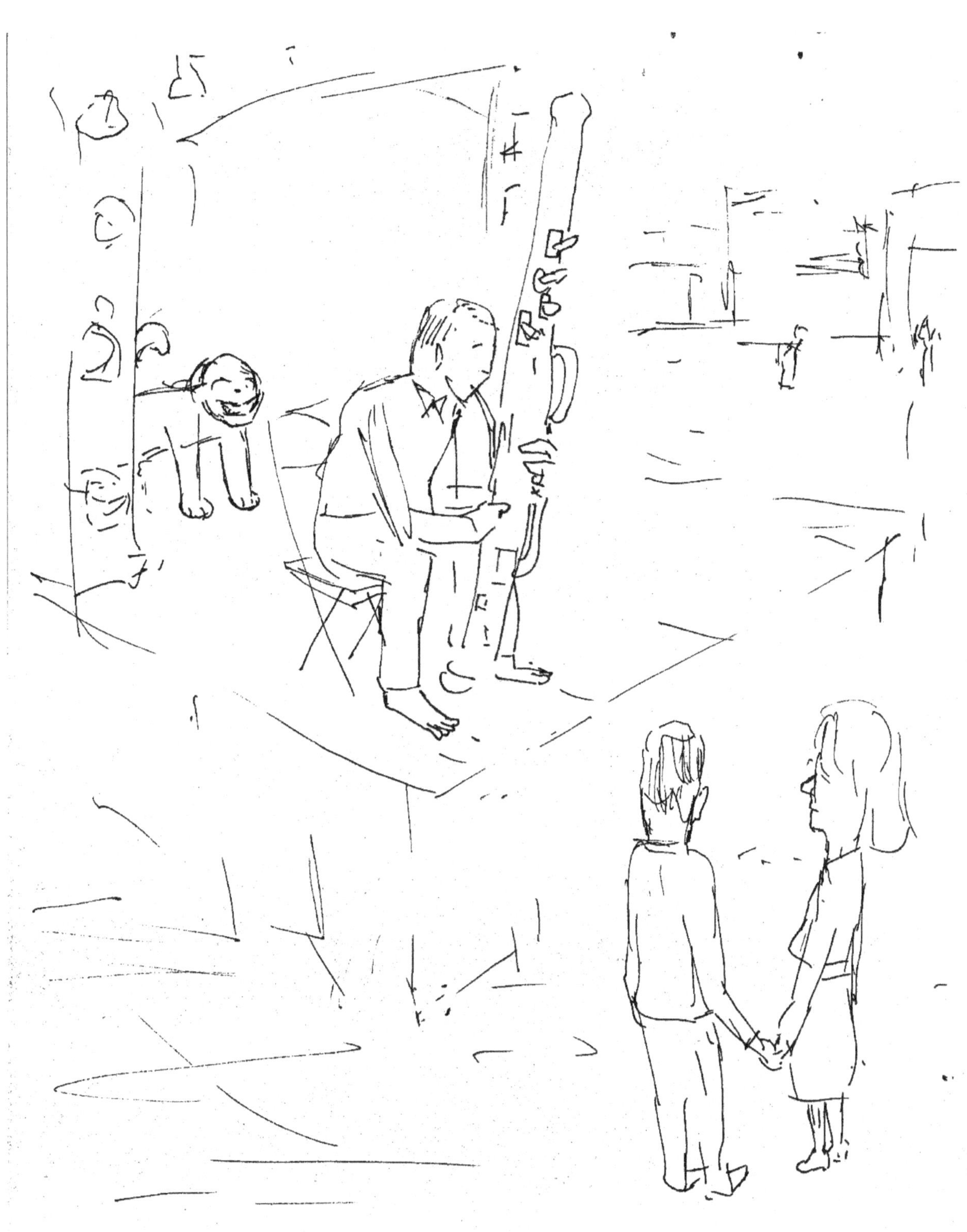

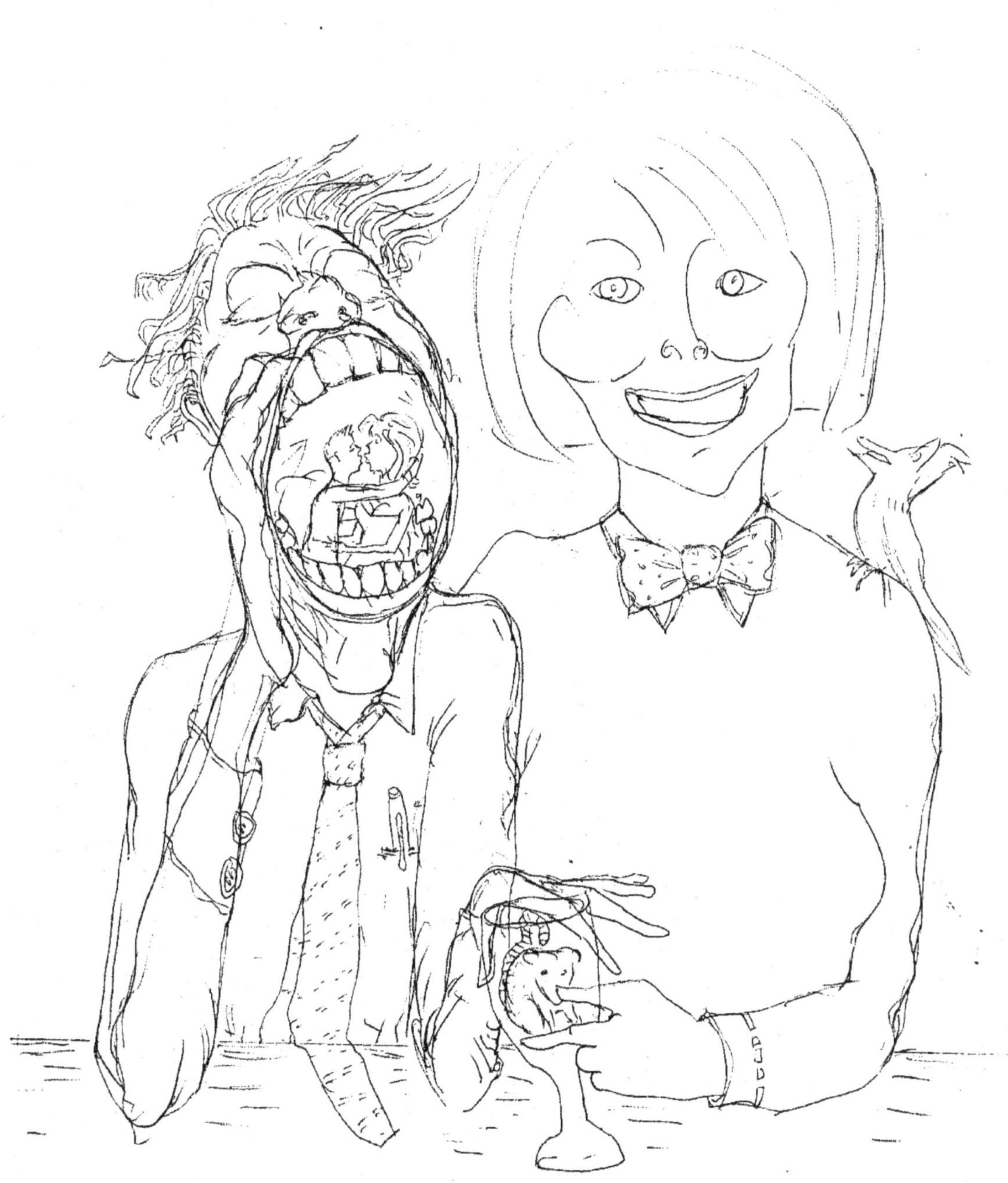

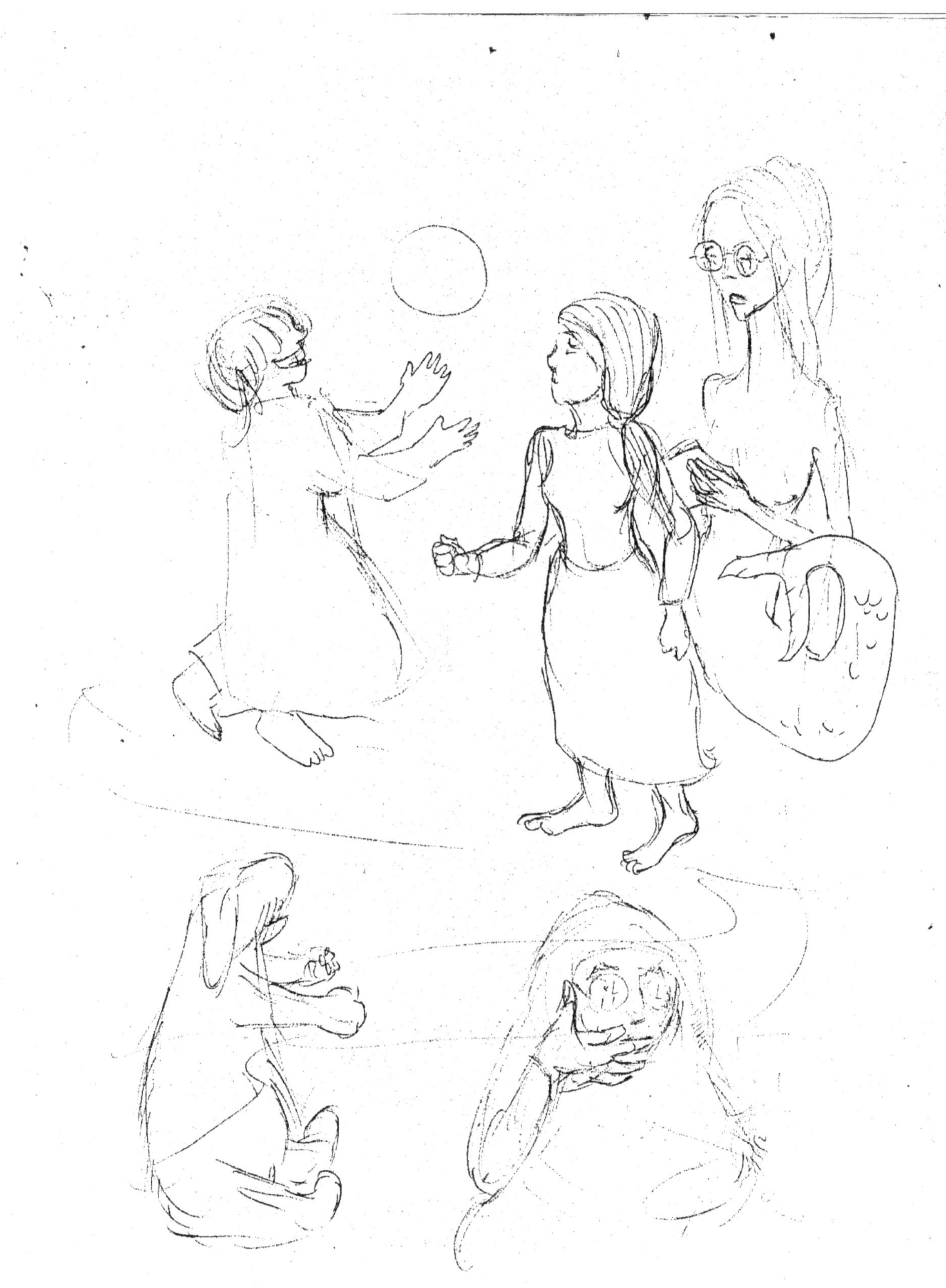

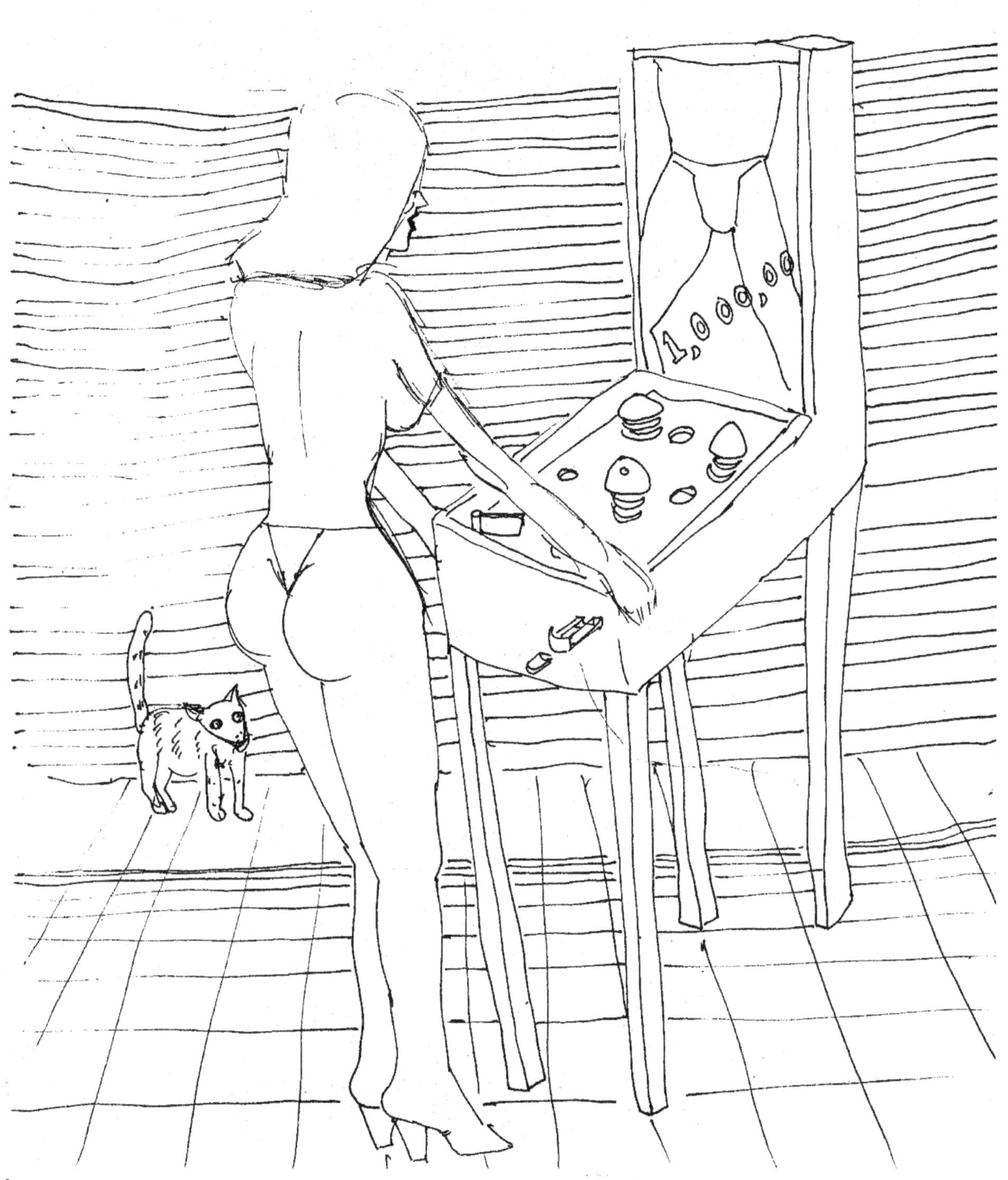

1,000,000

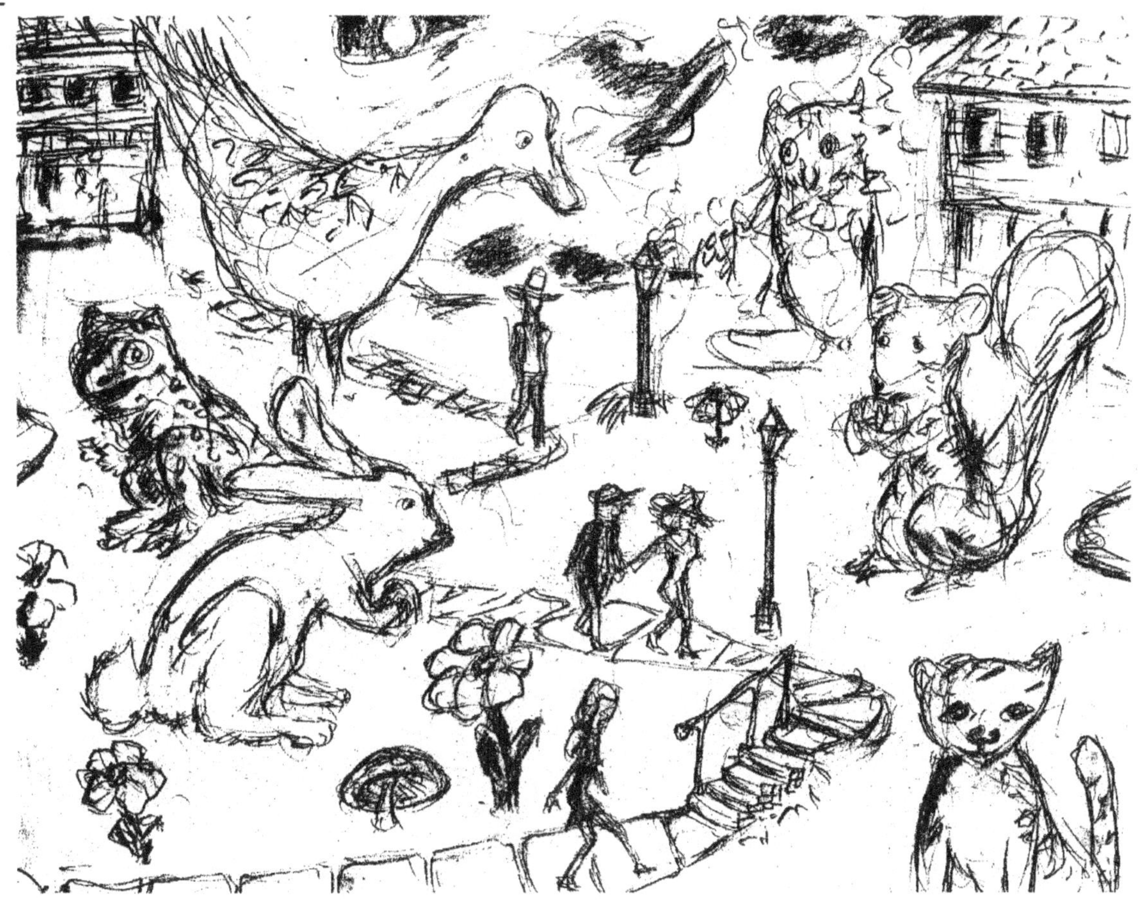

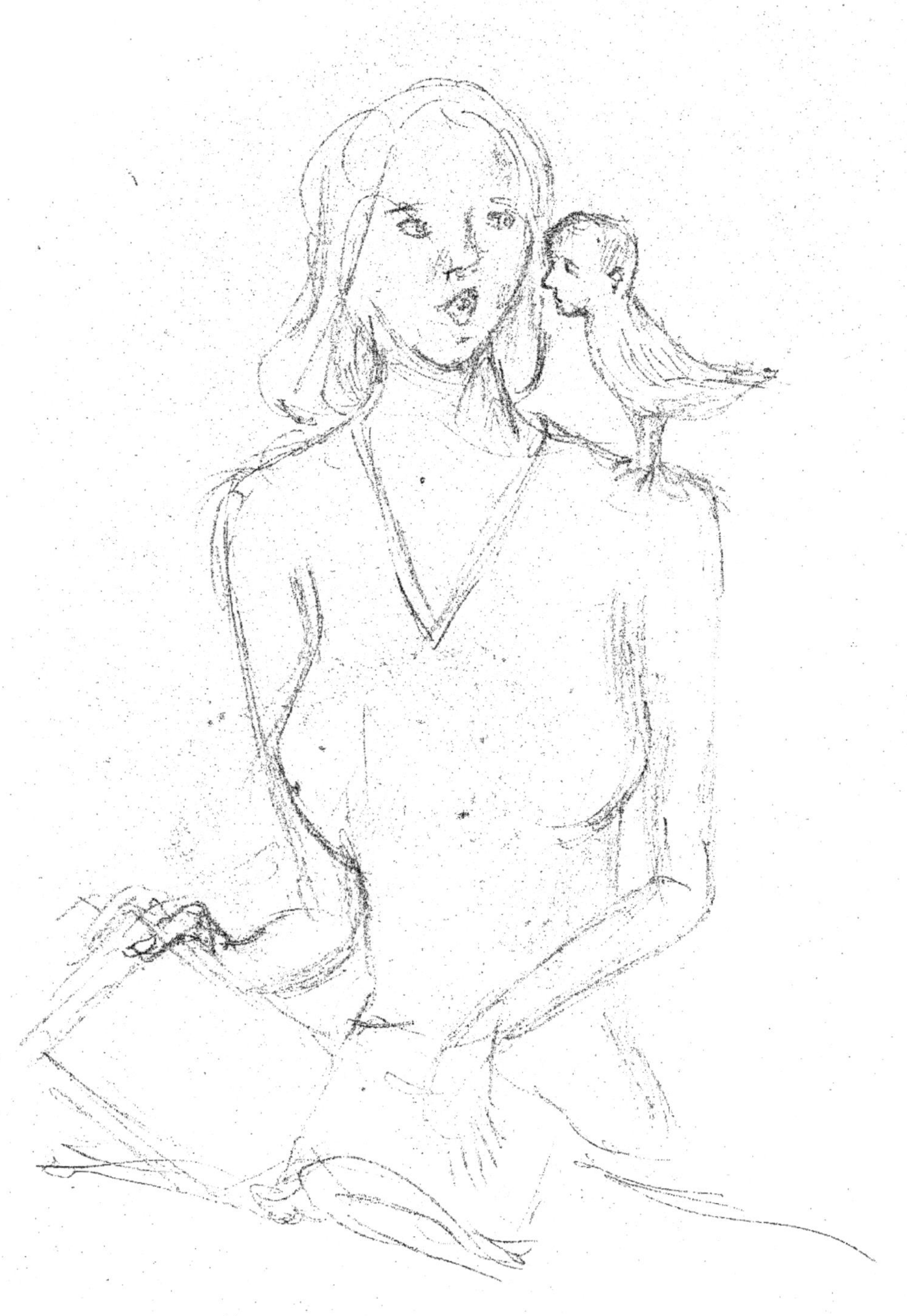

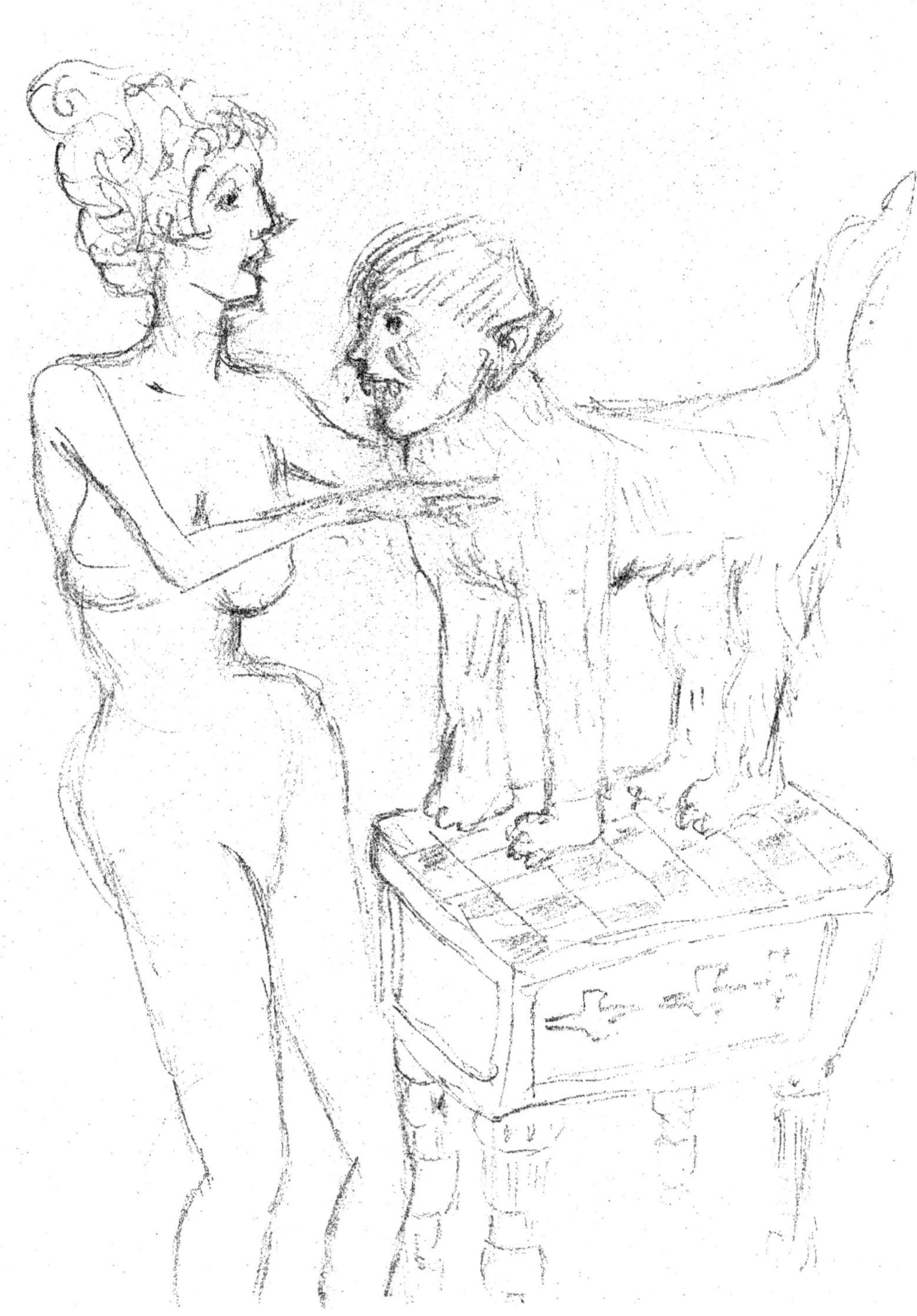

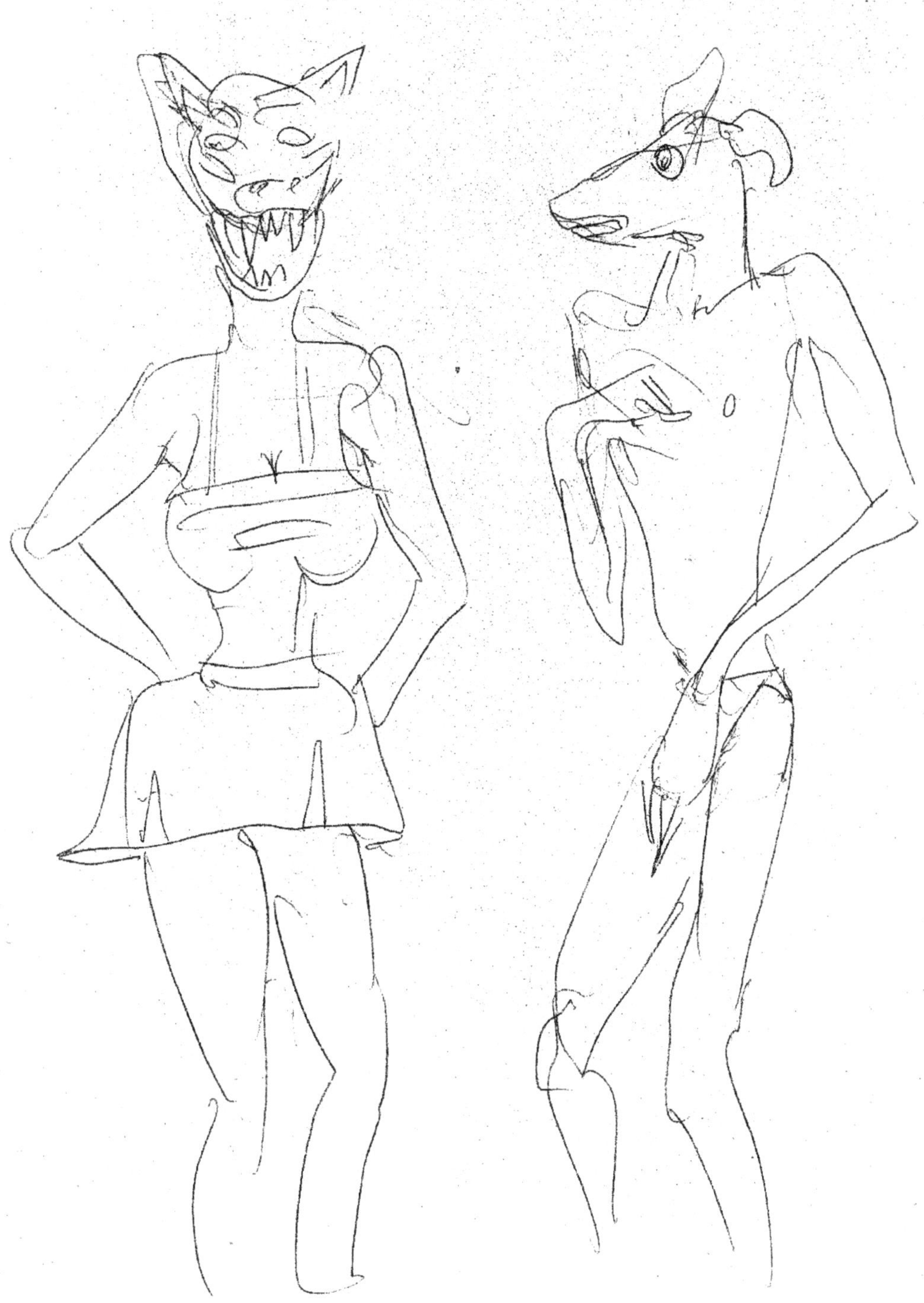

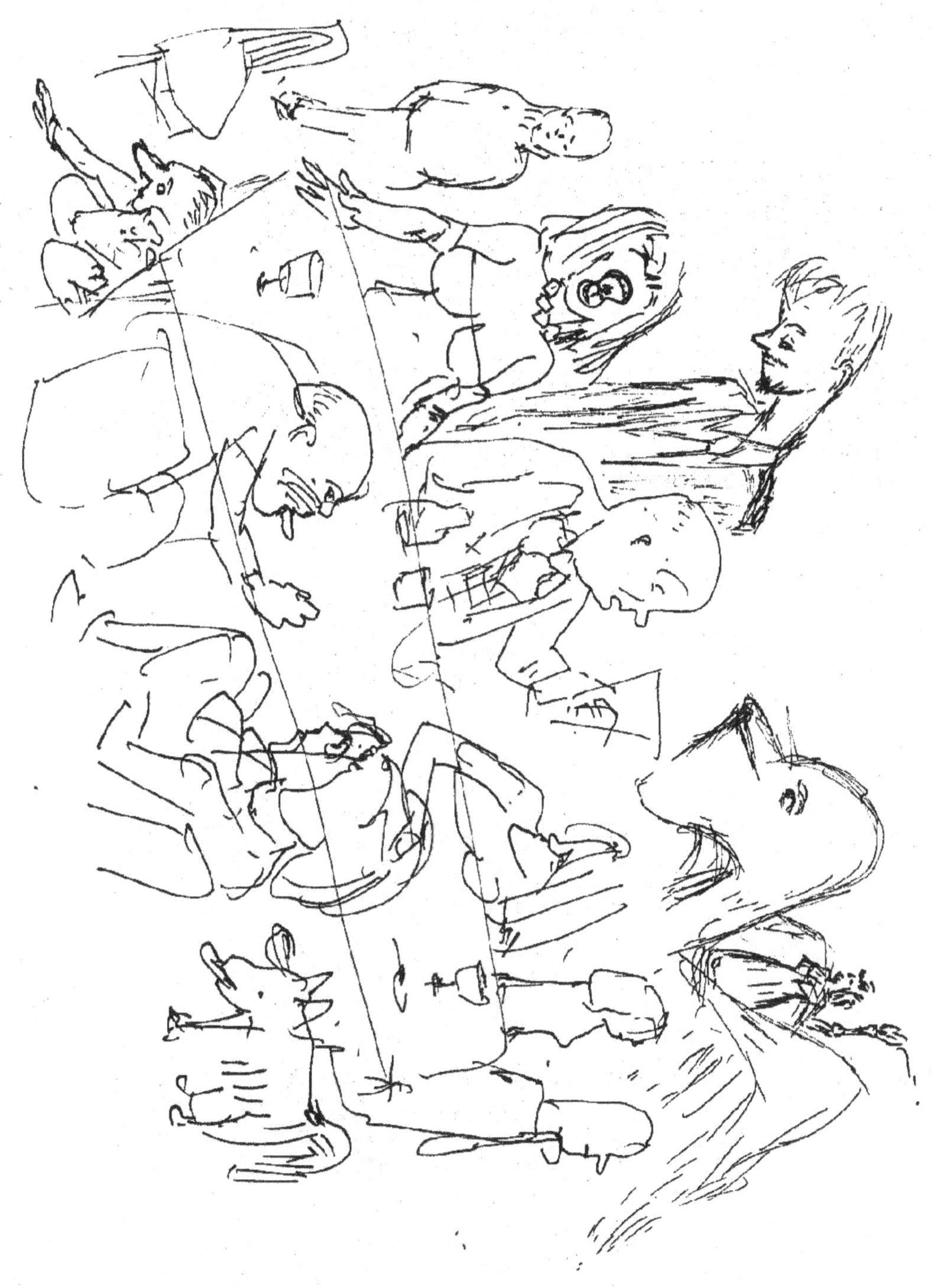

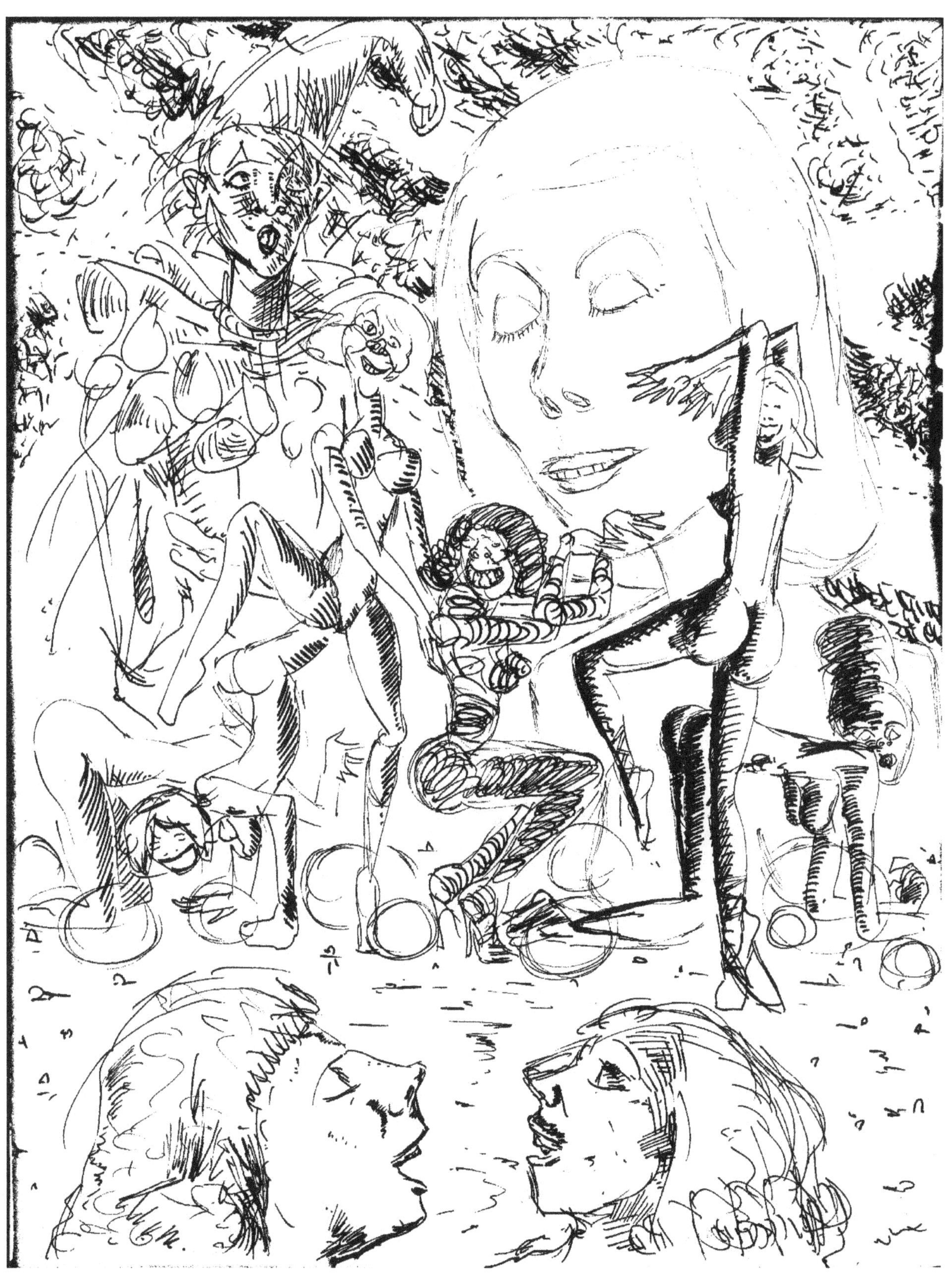

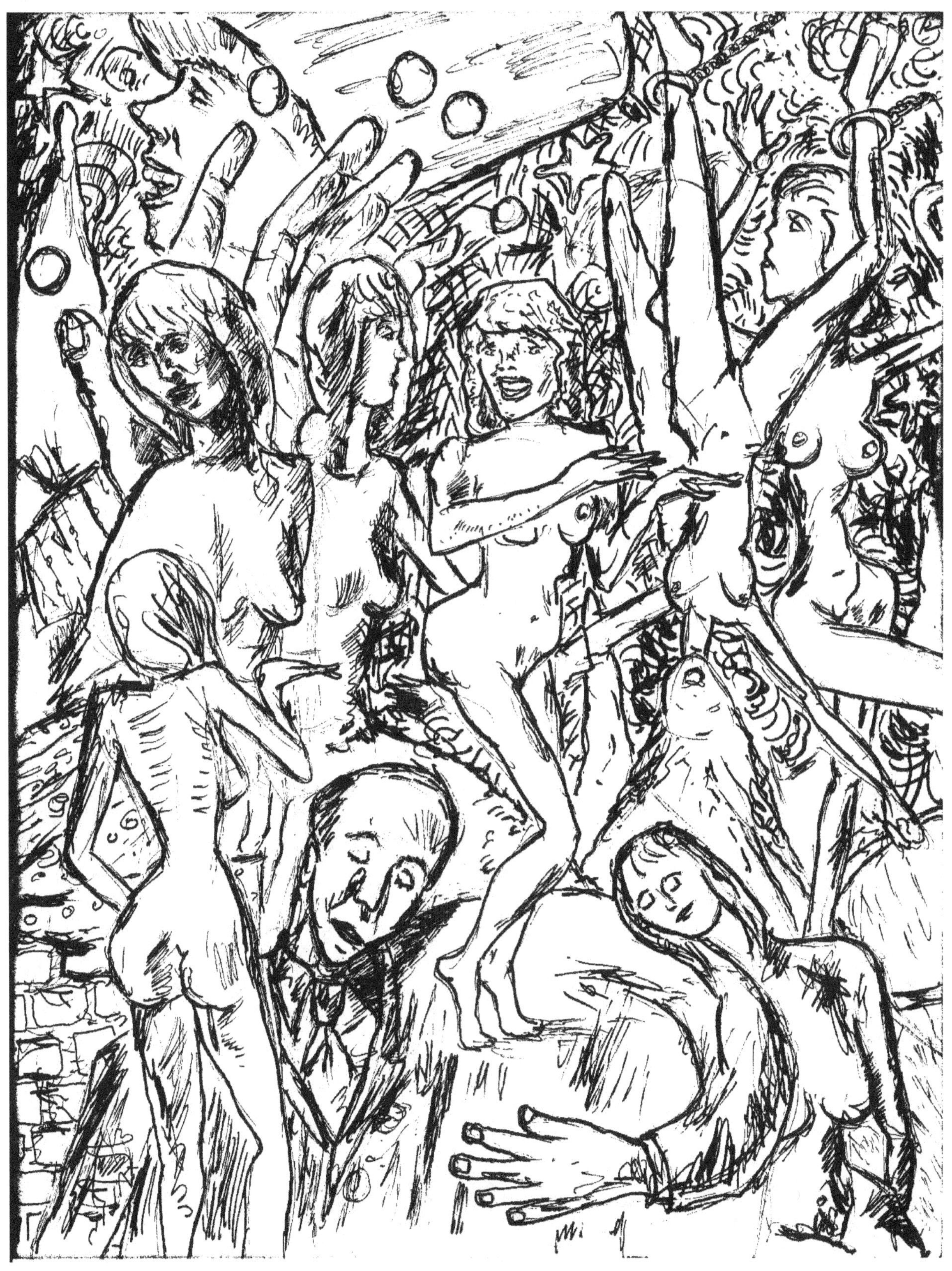

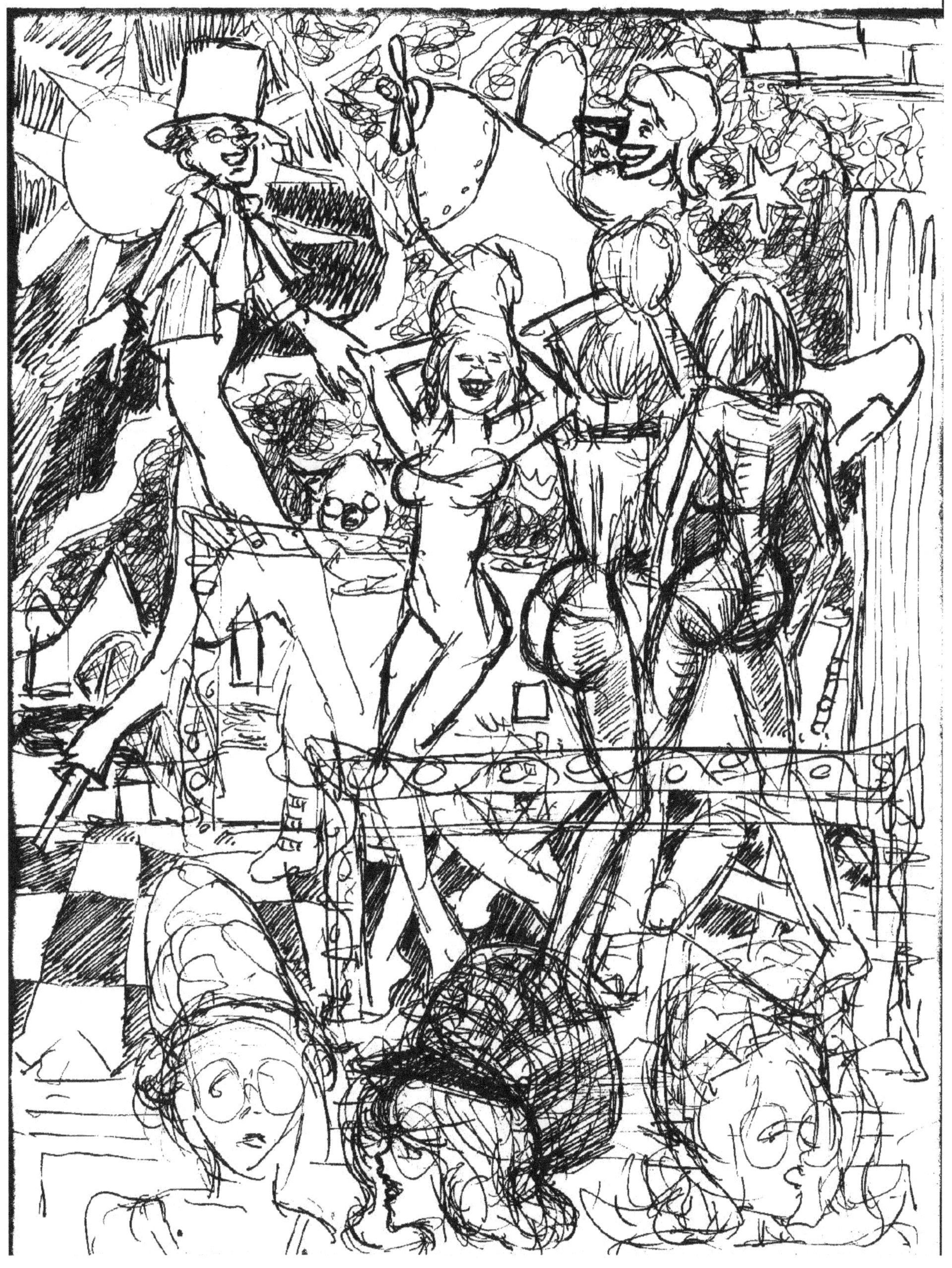

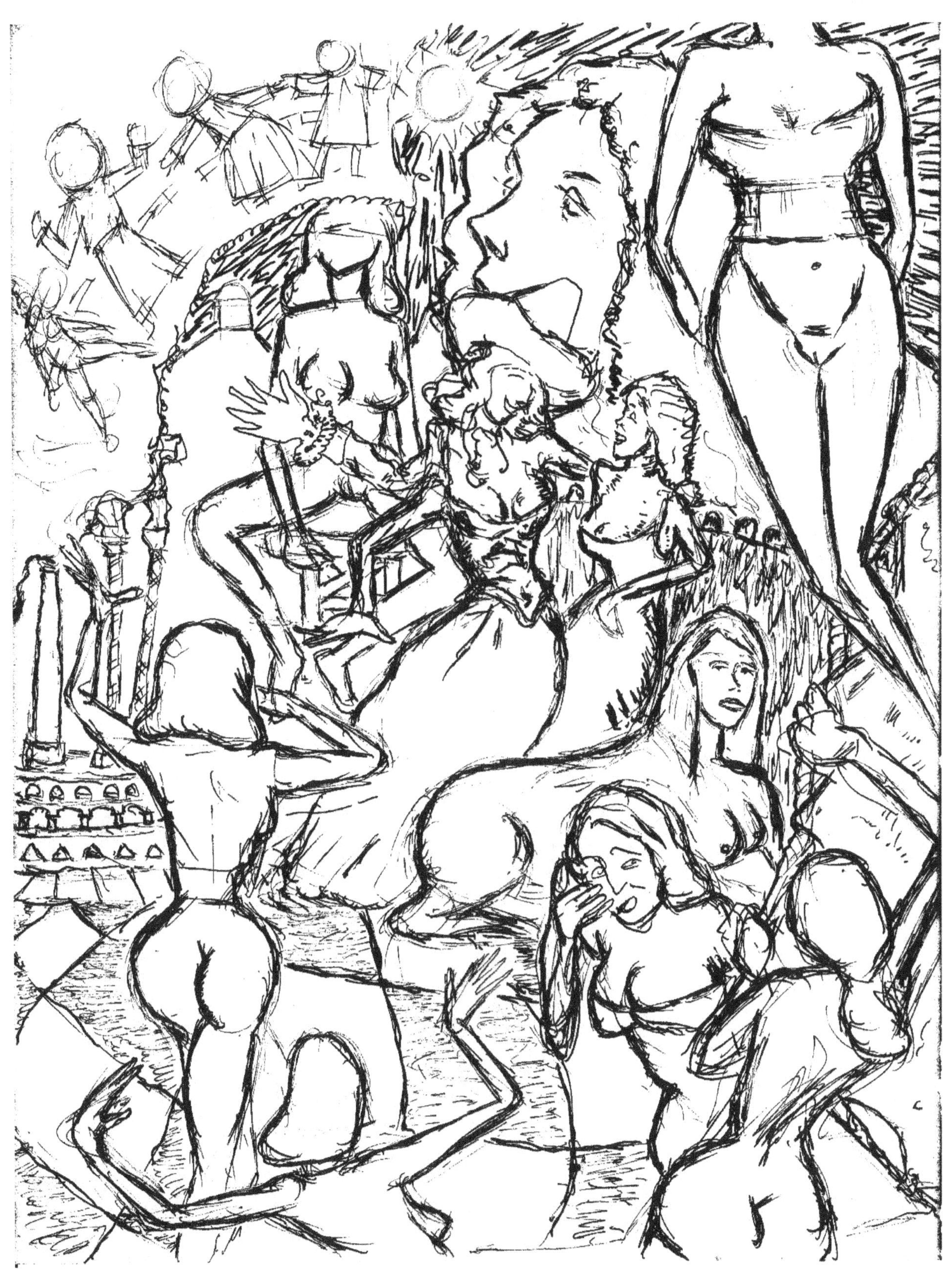

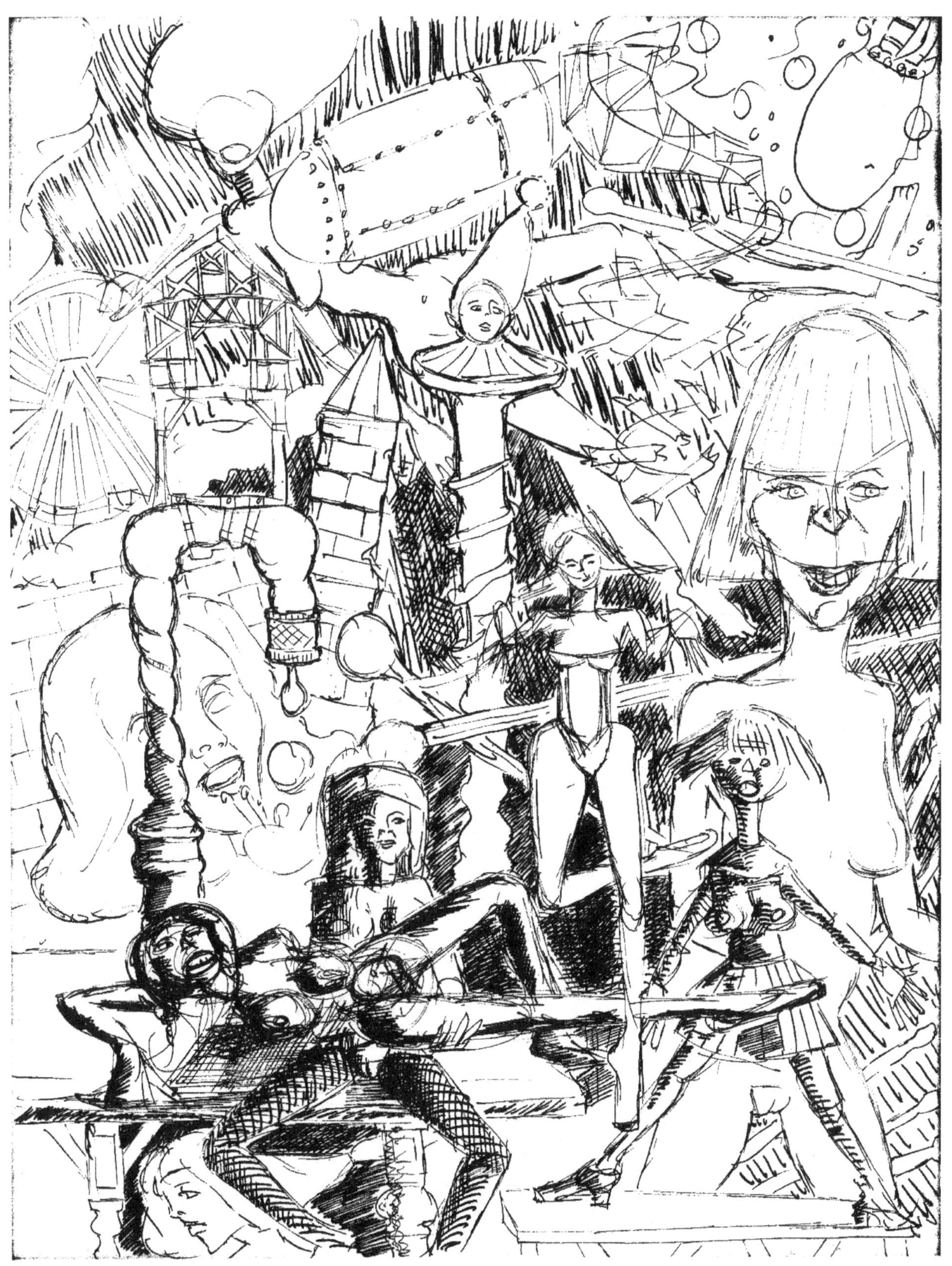

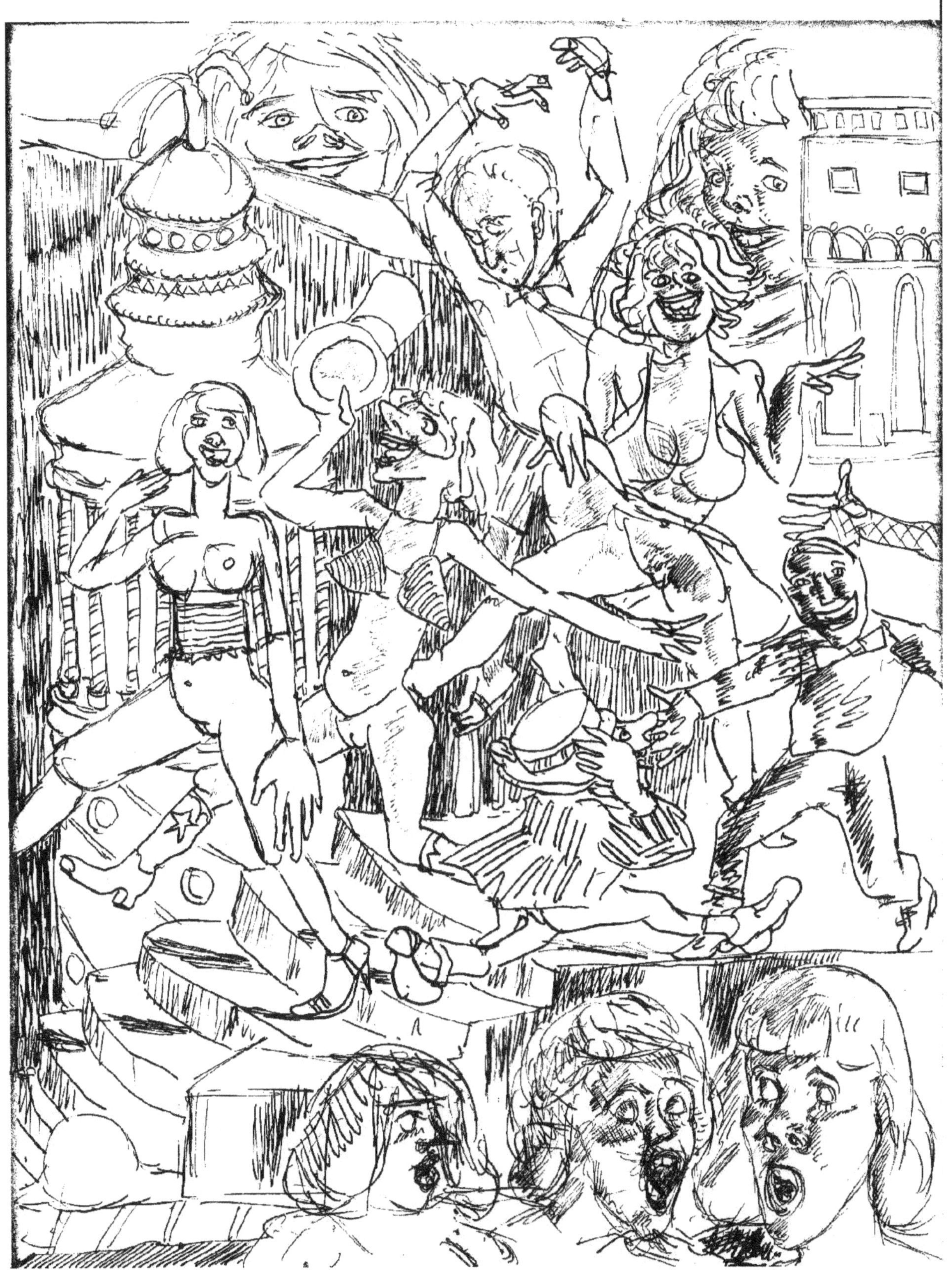

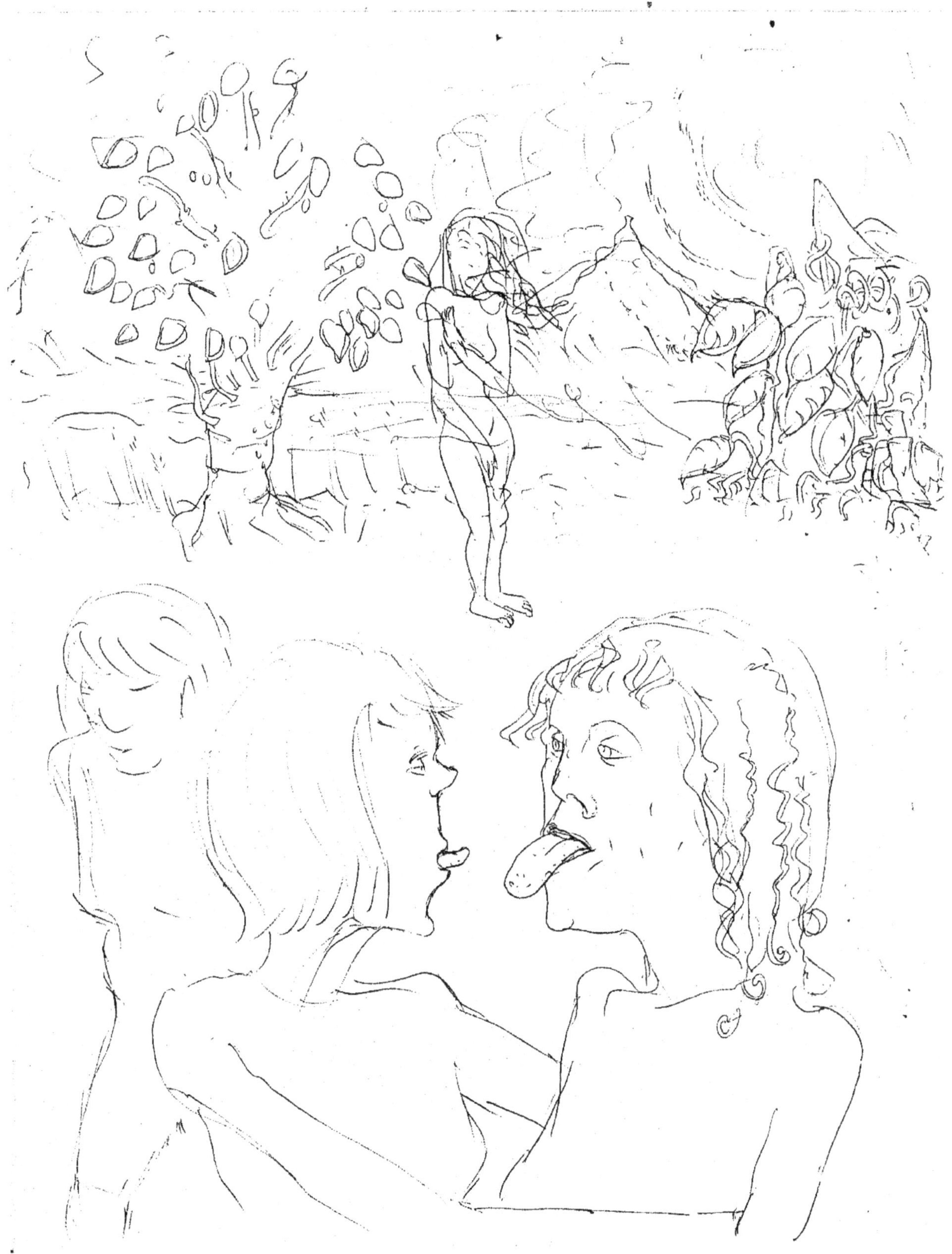

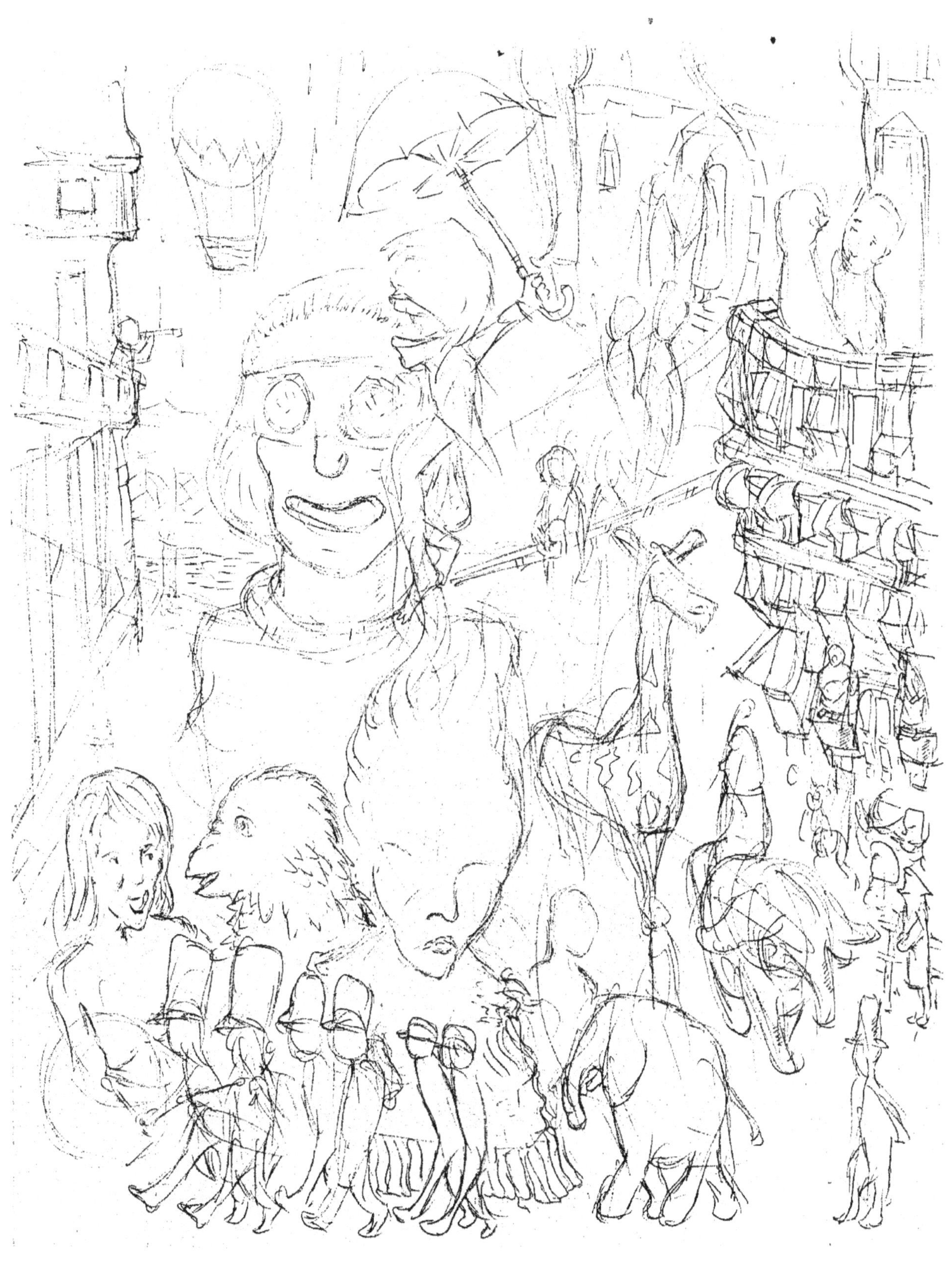

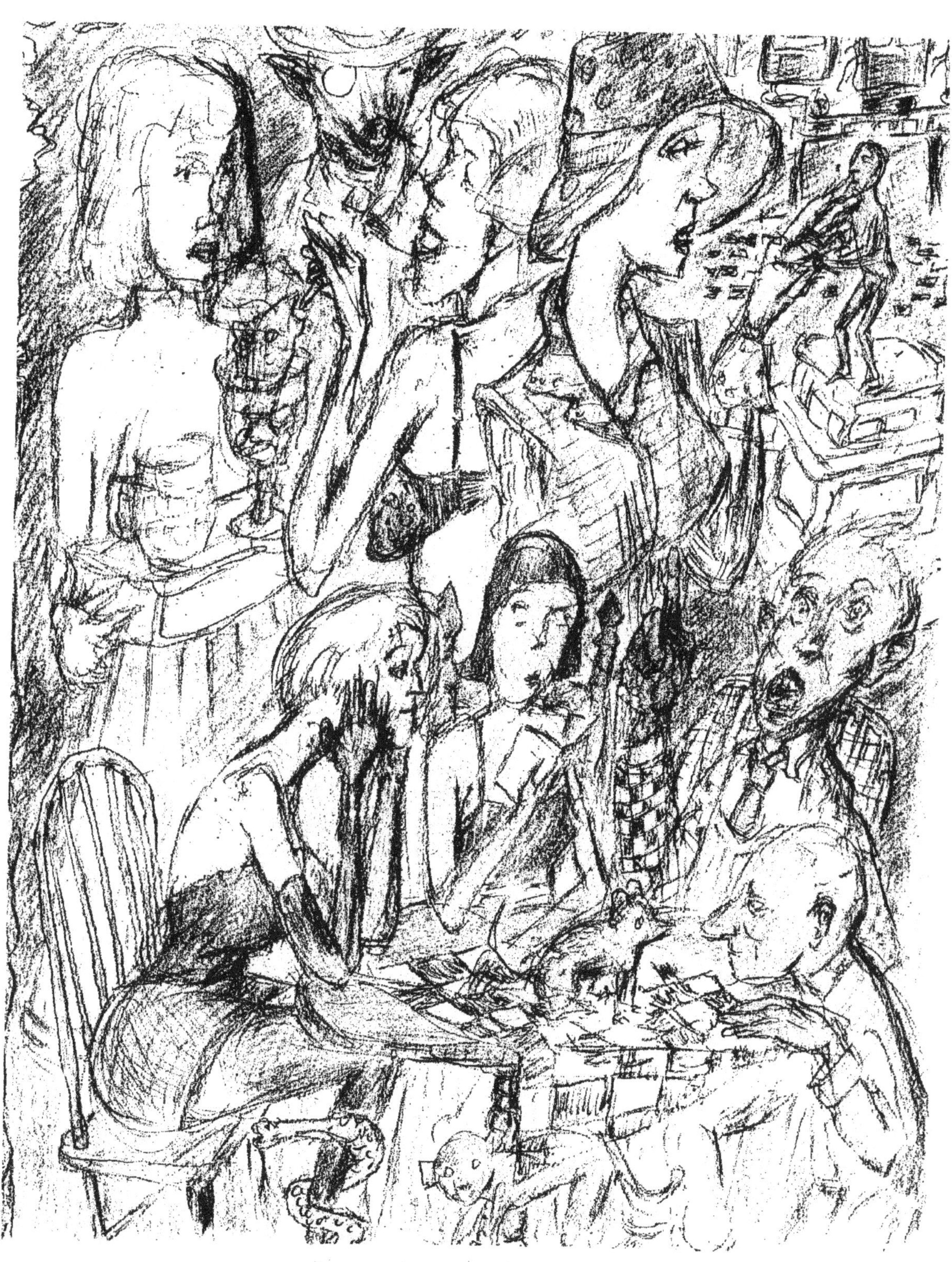

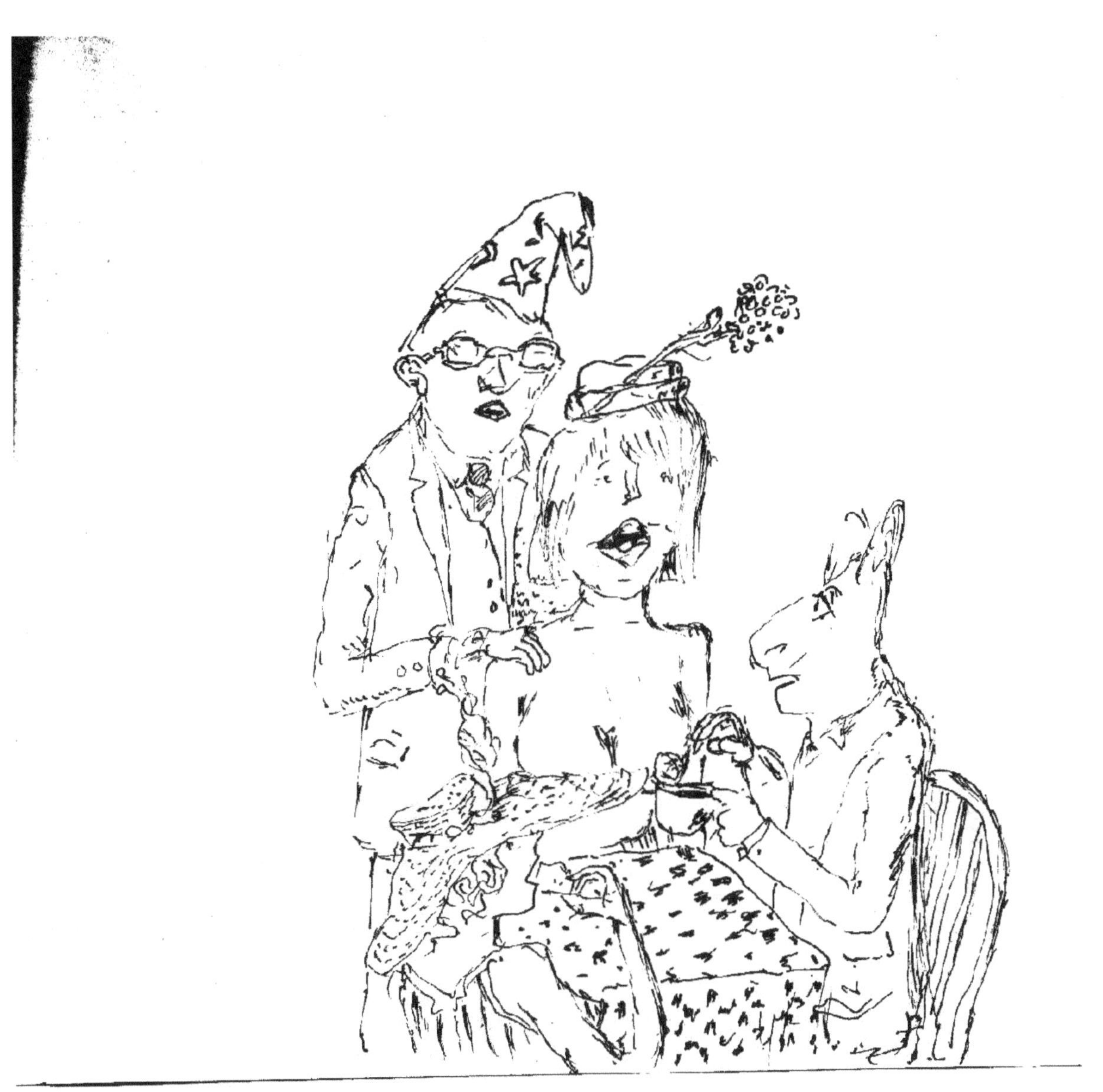

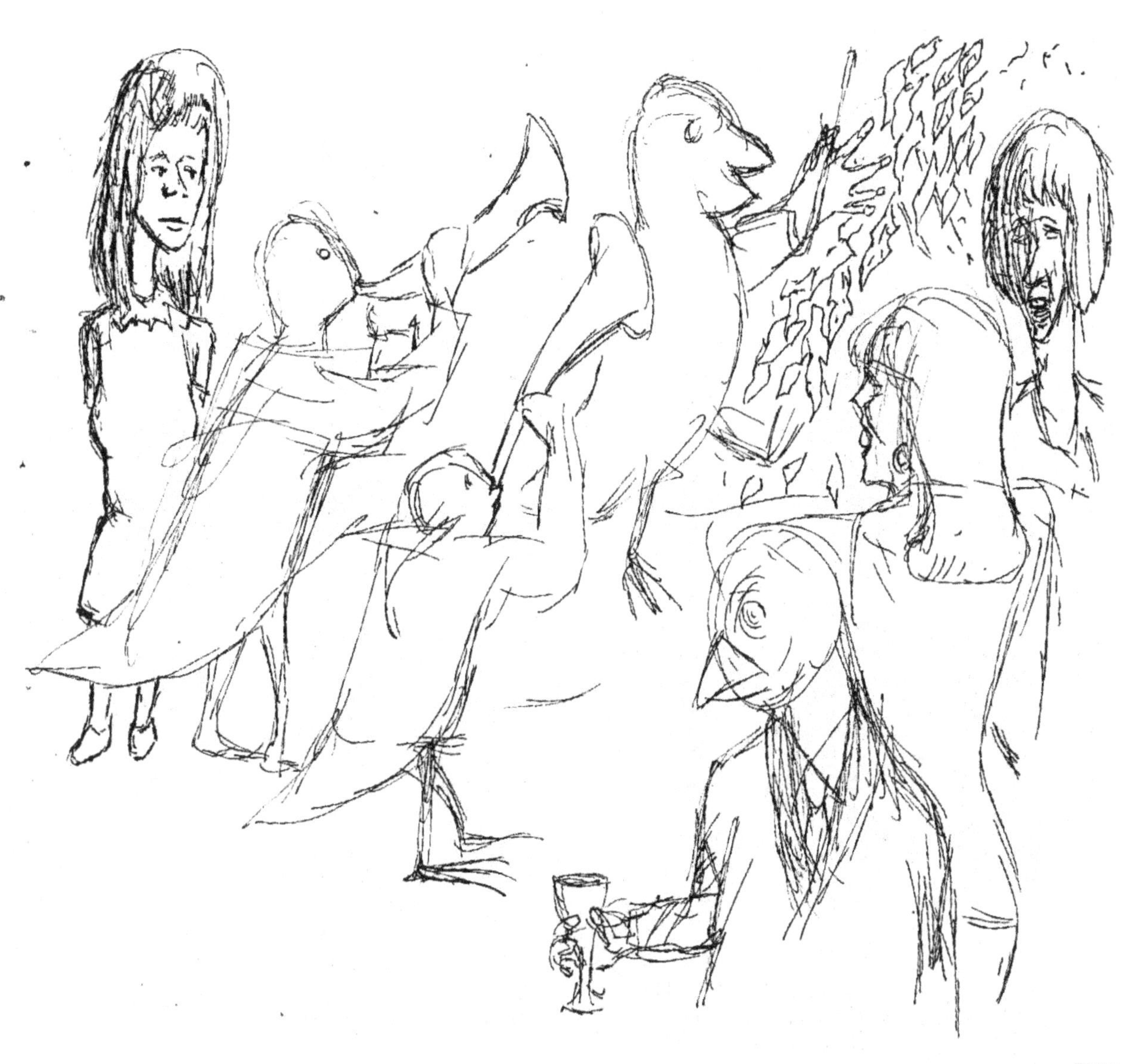

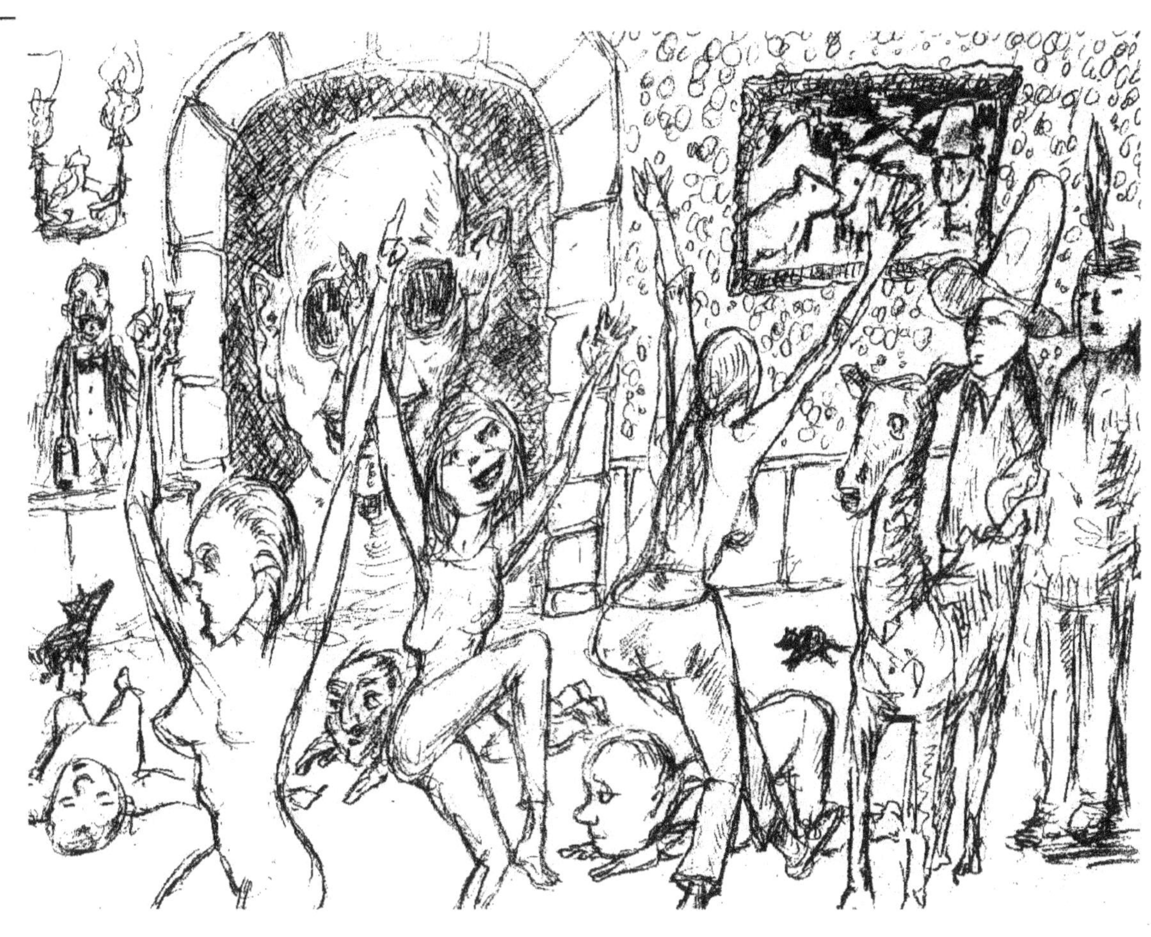

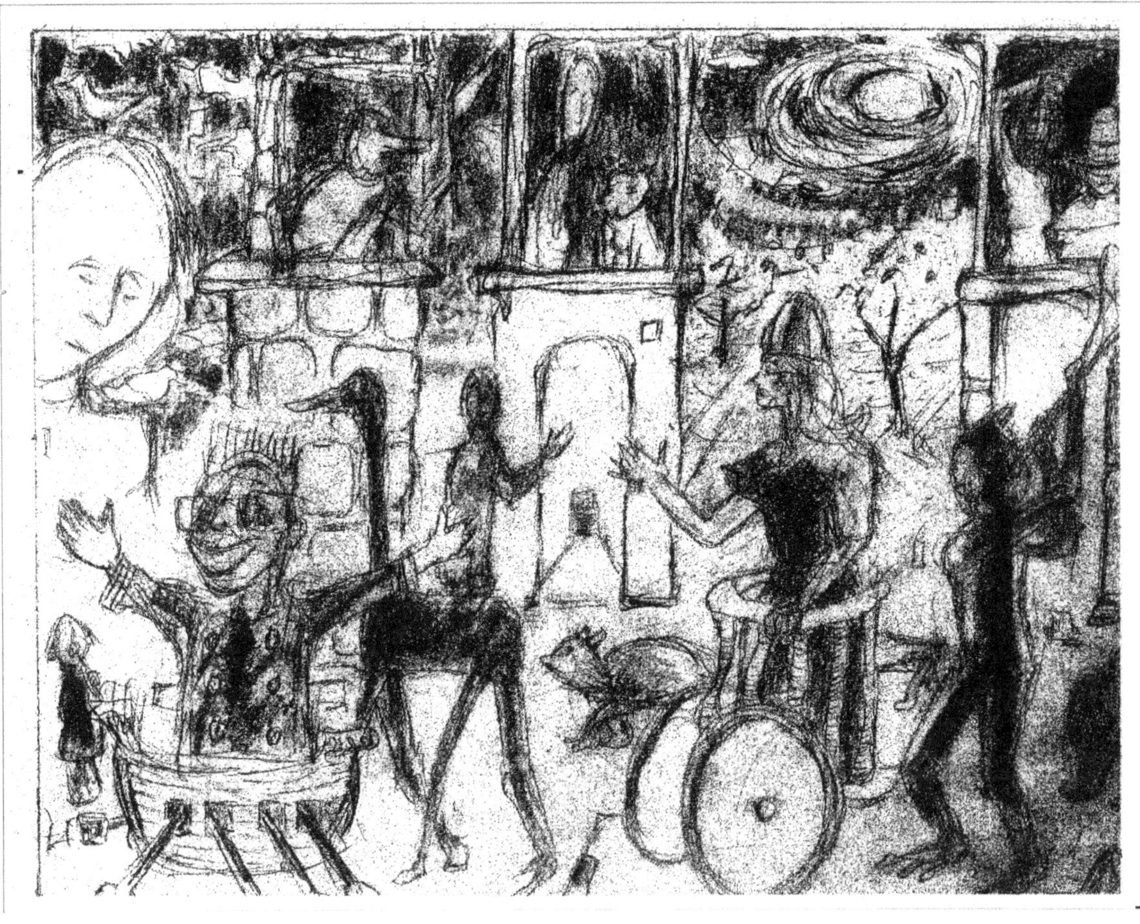

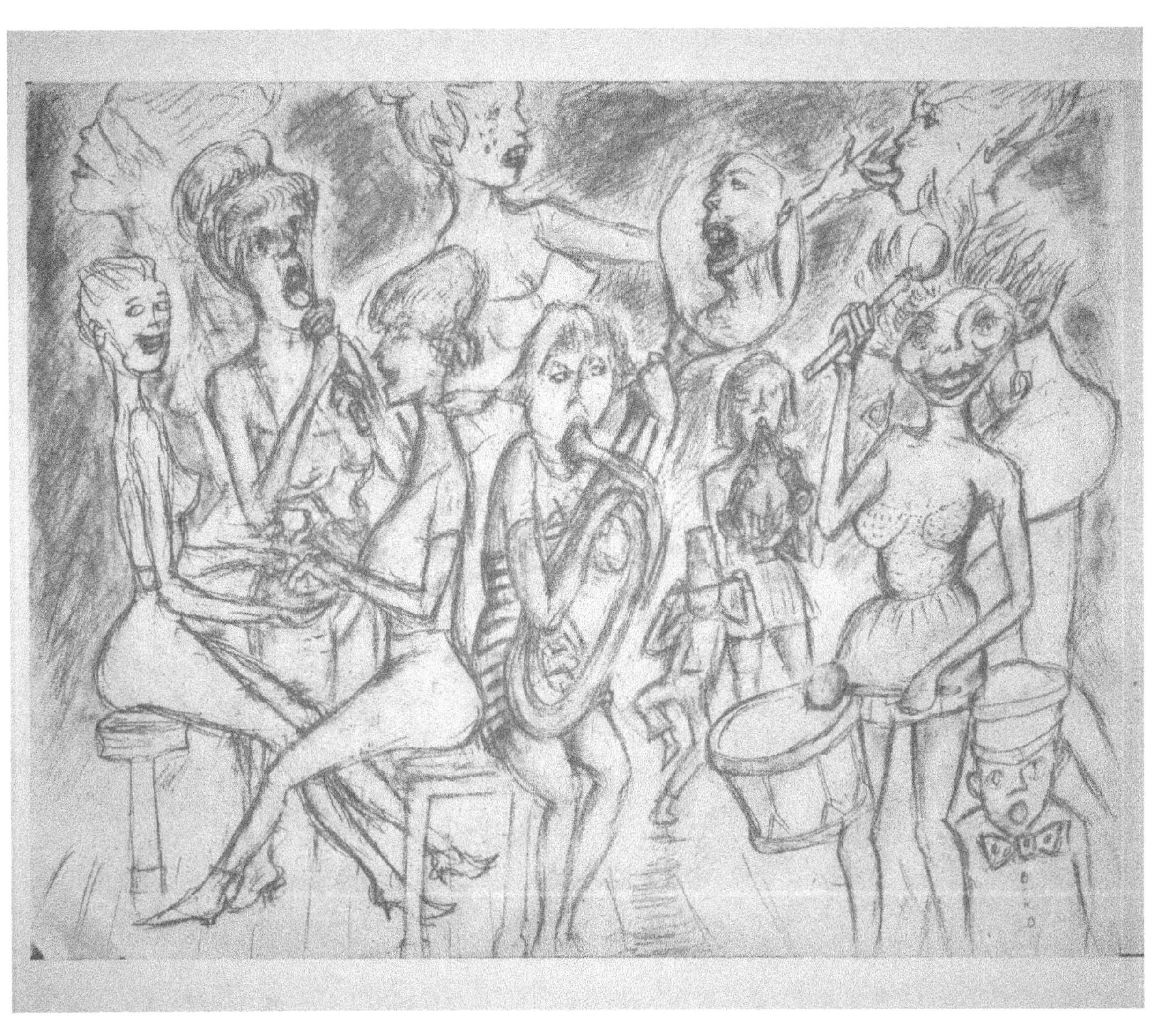

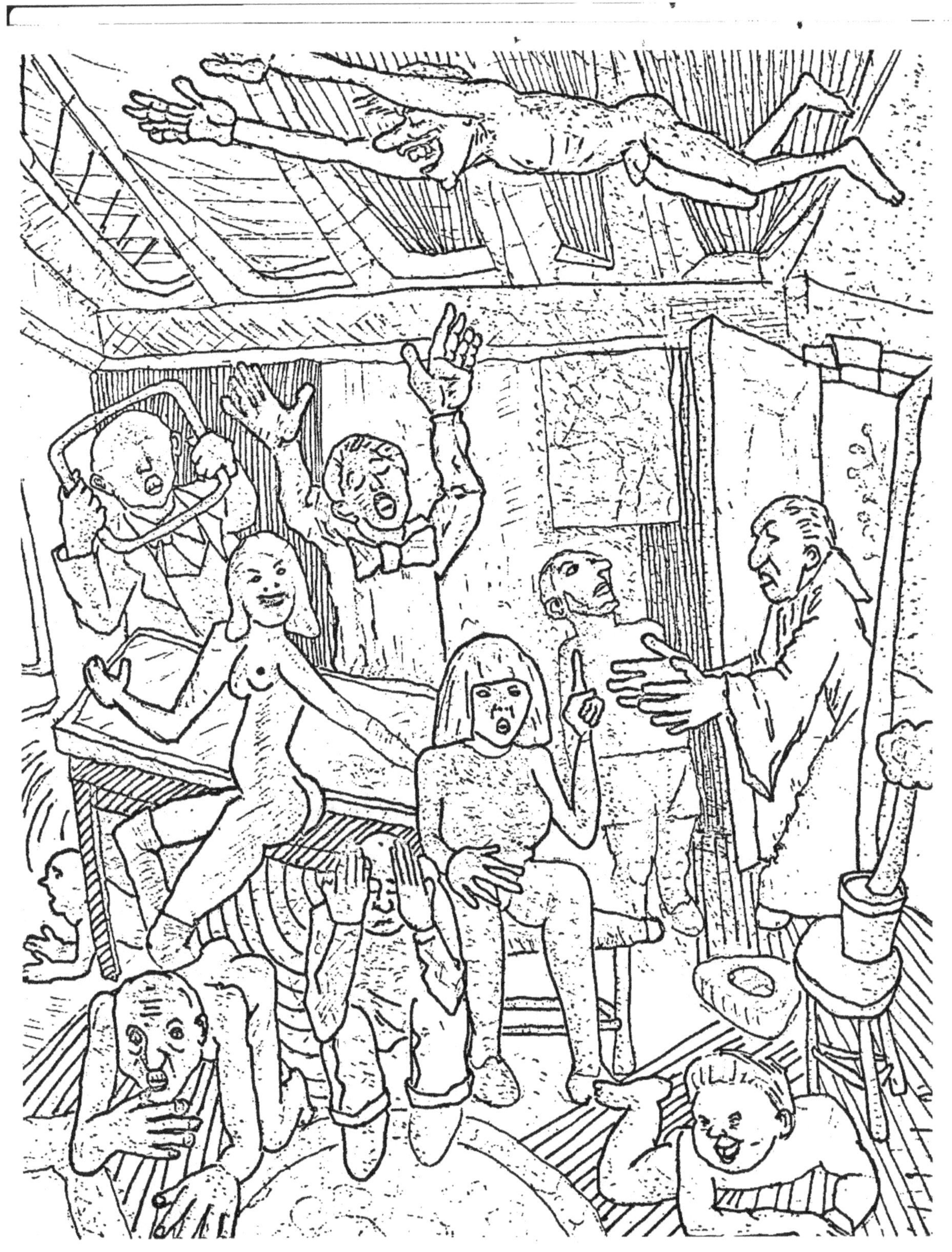

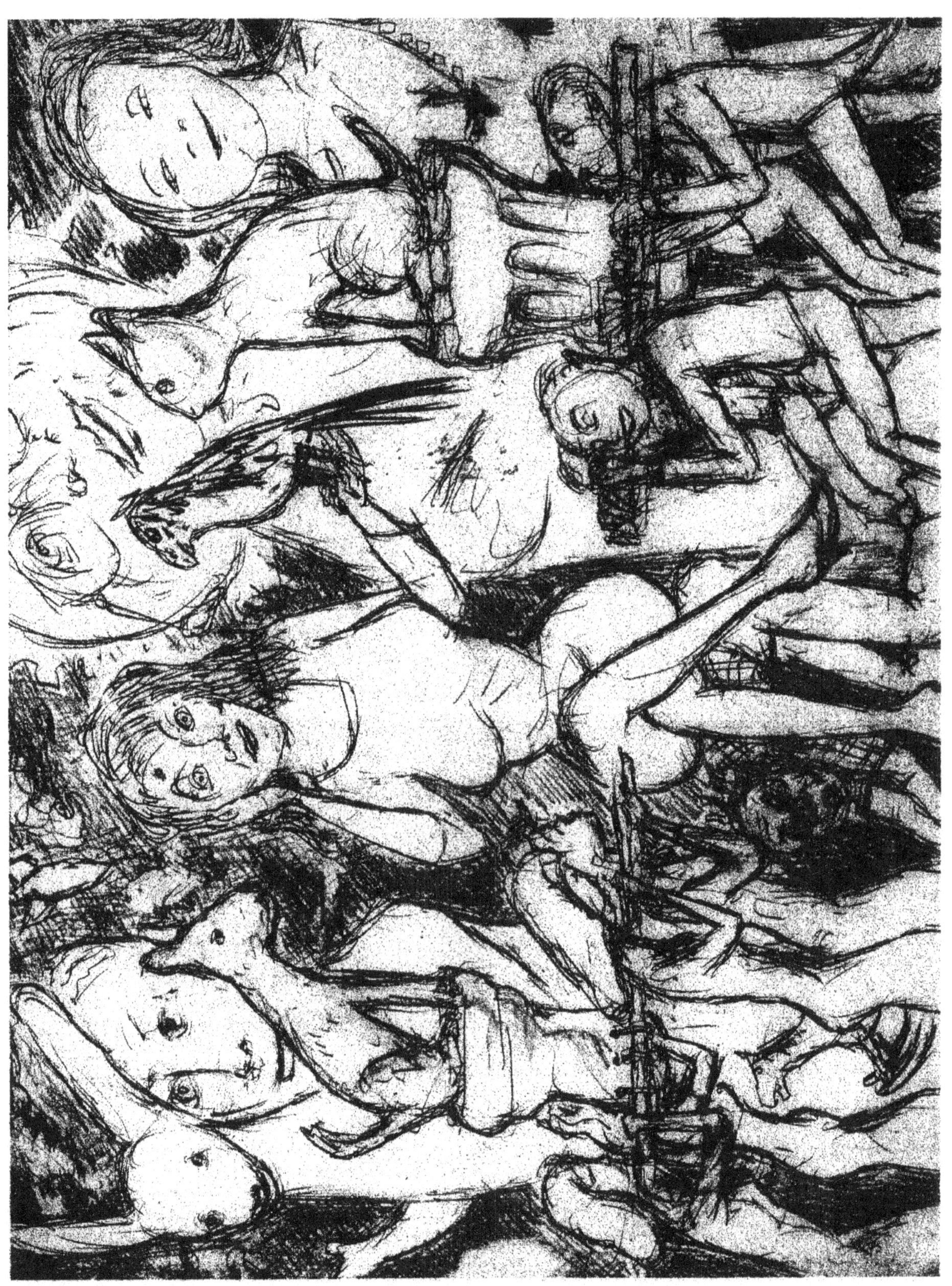

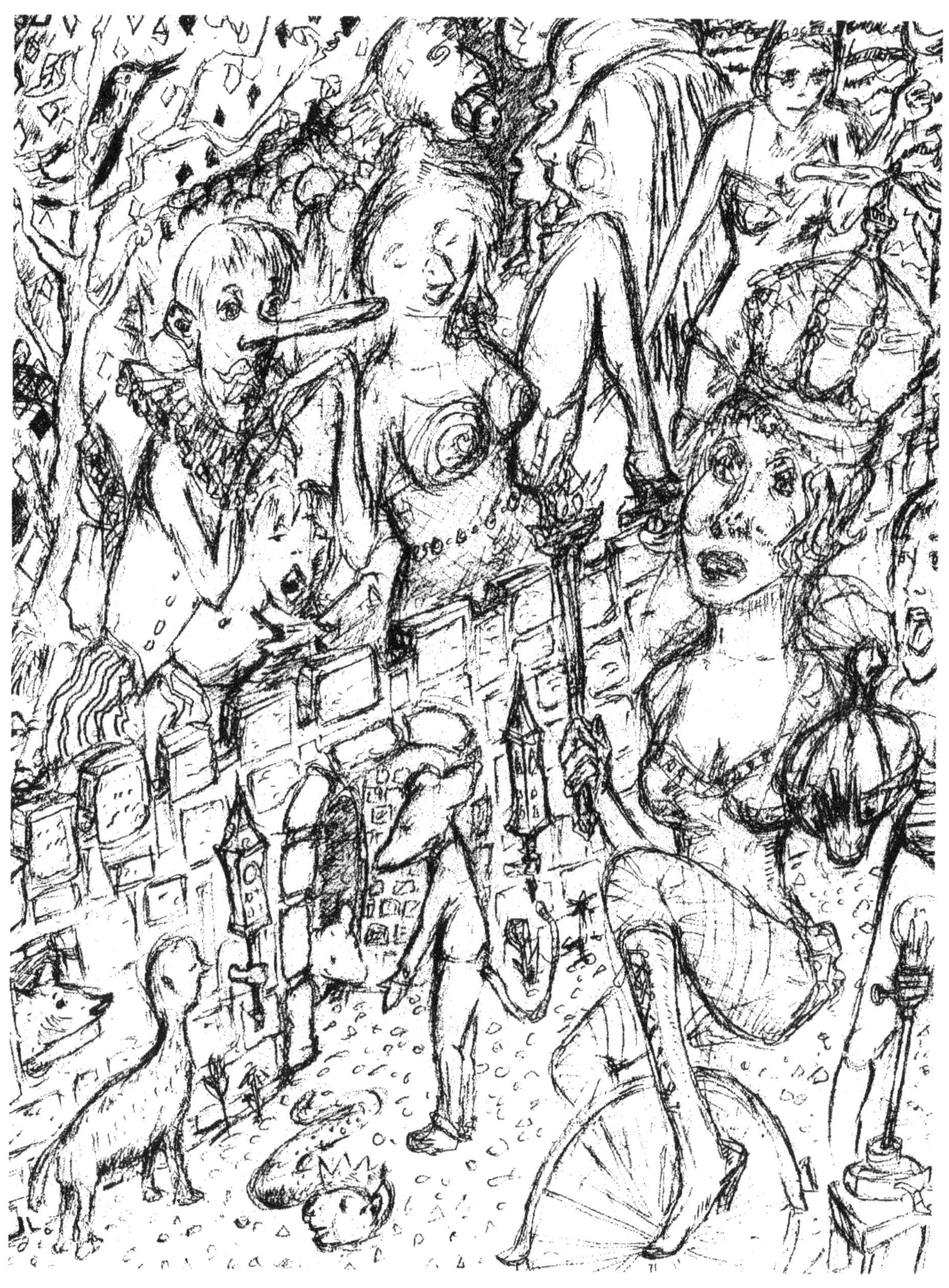

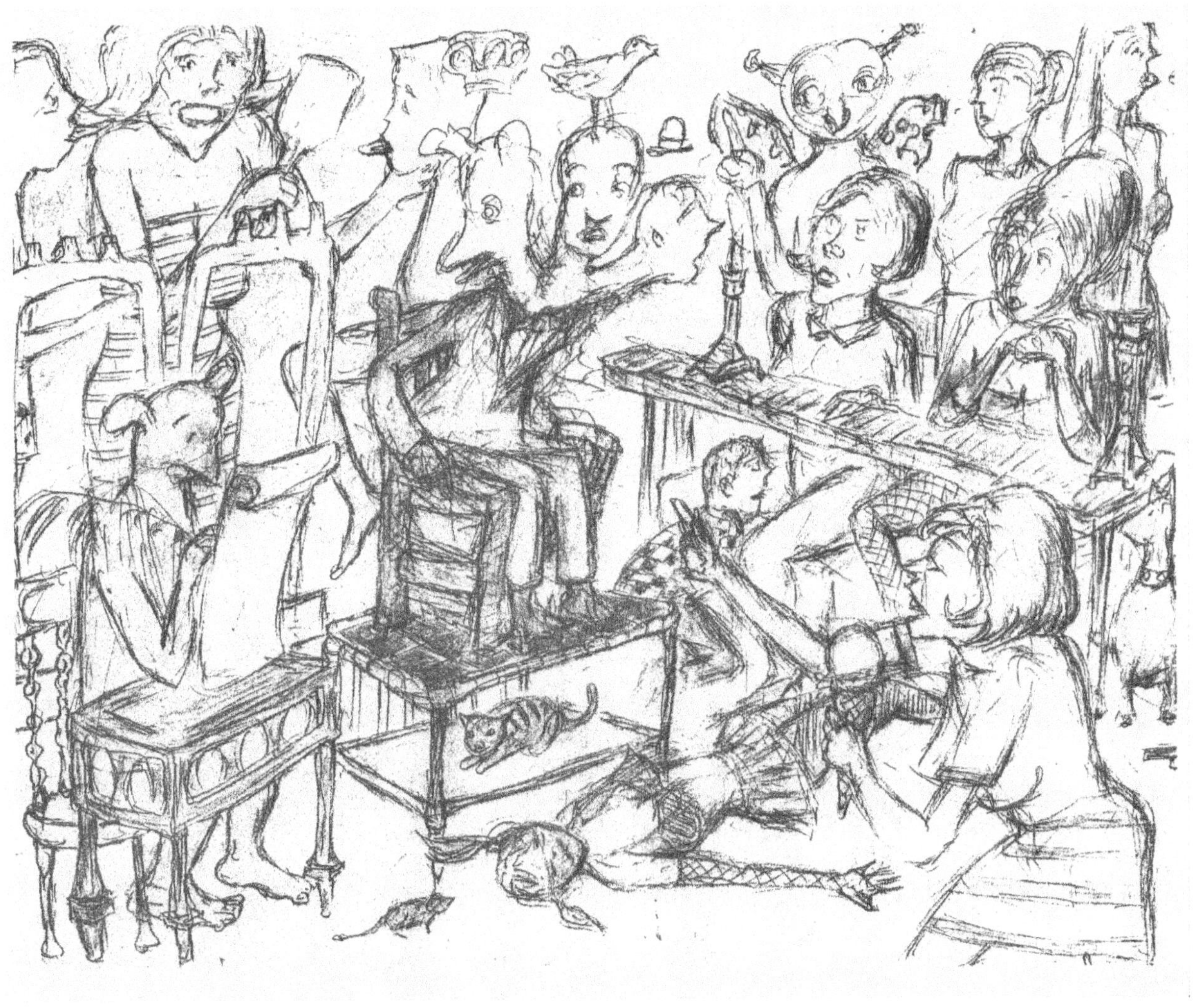

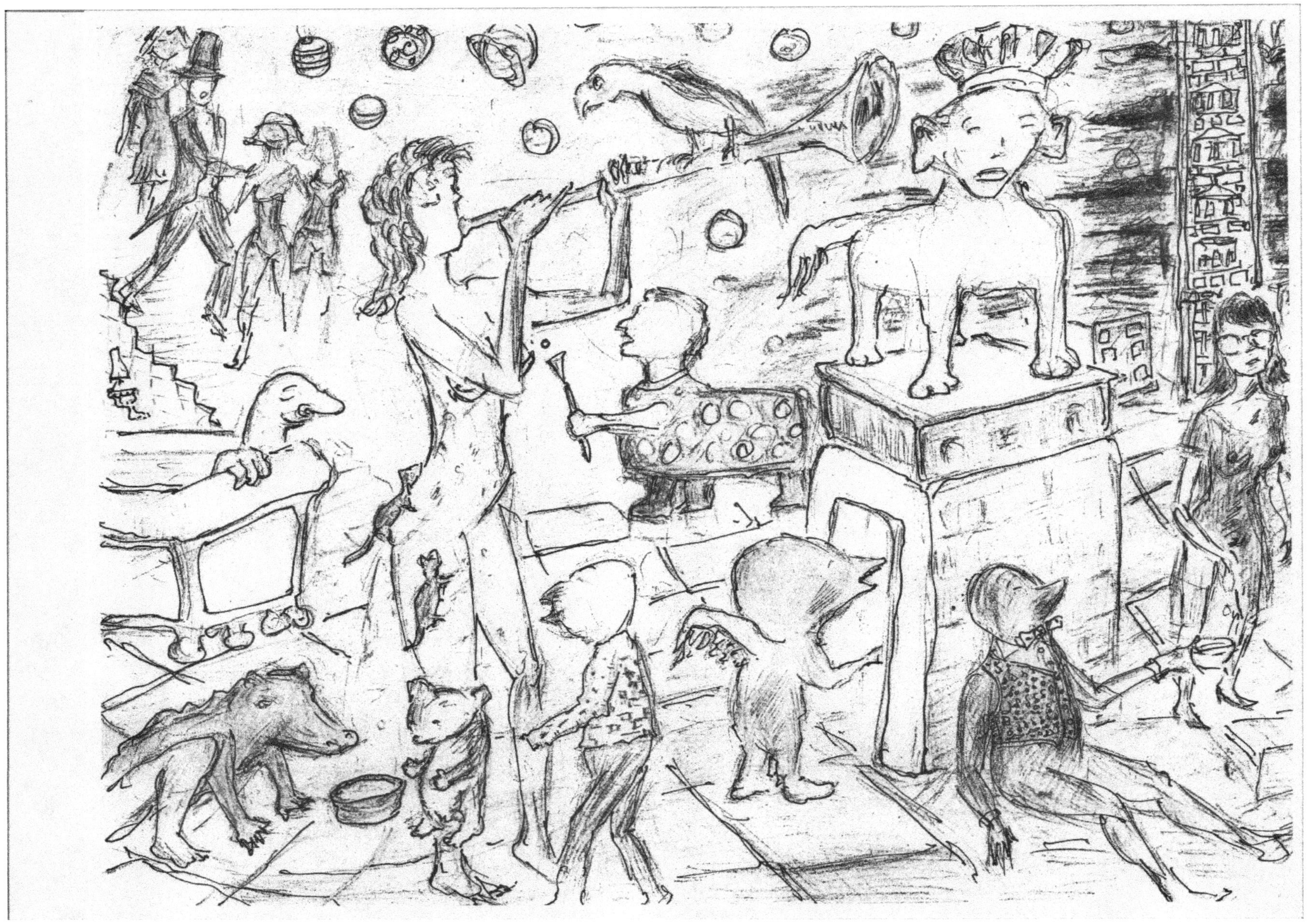

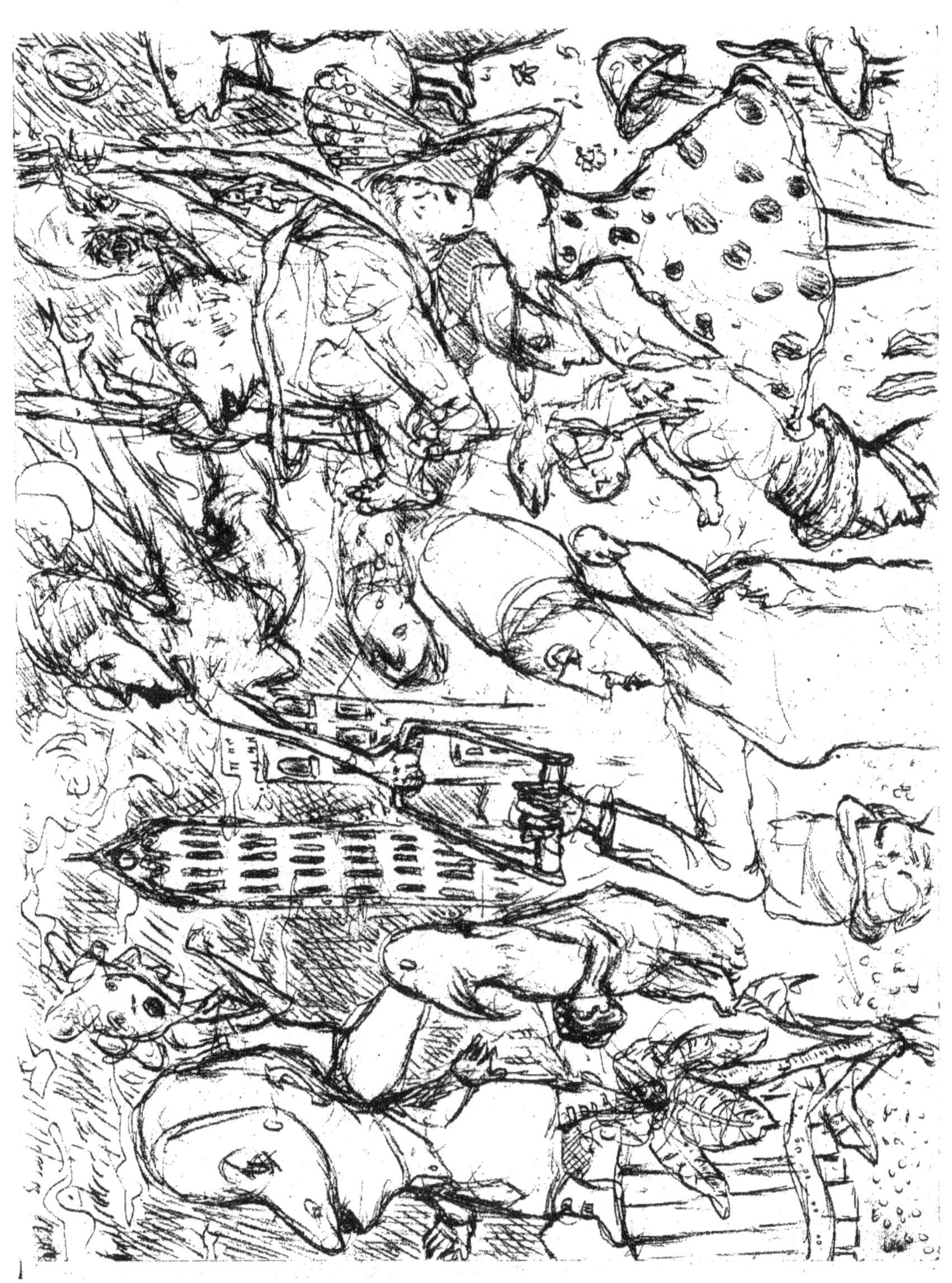

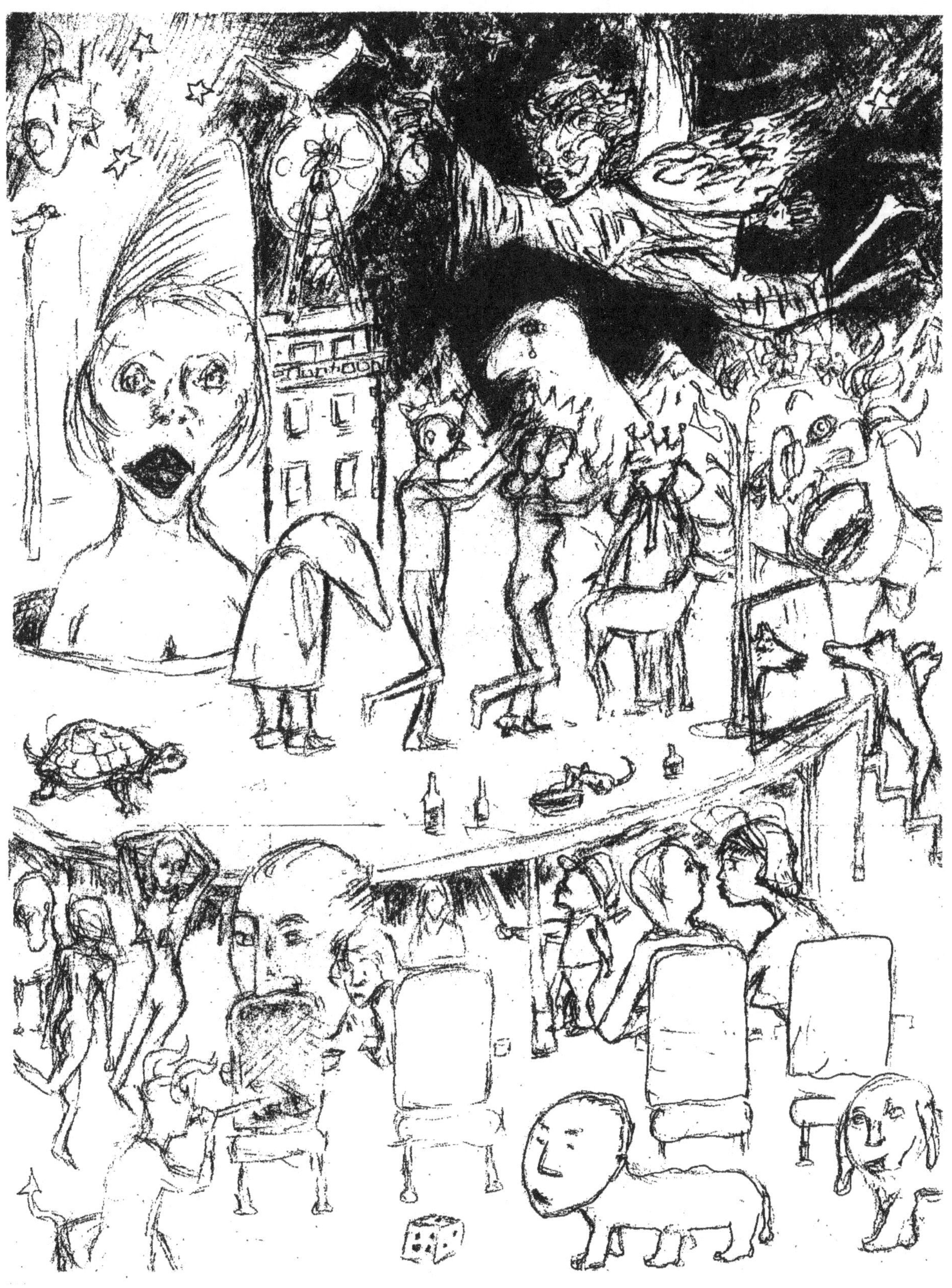

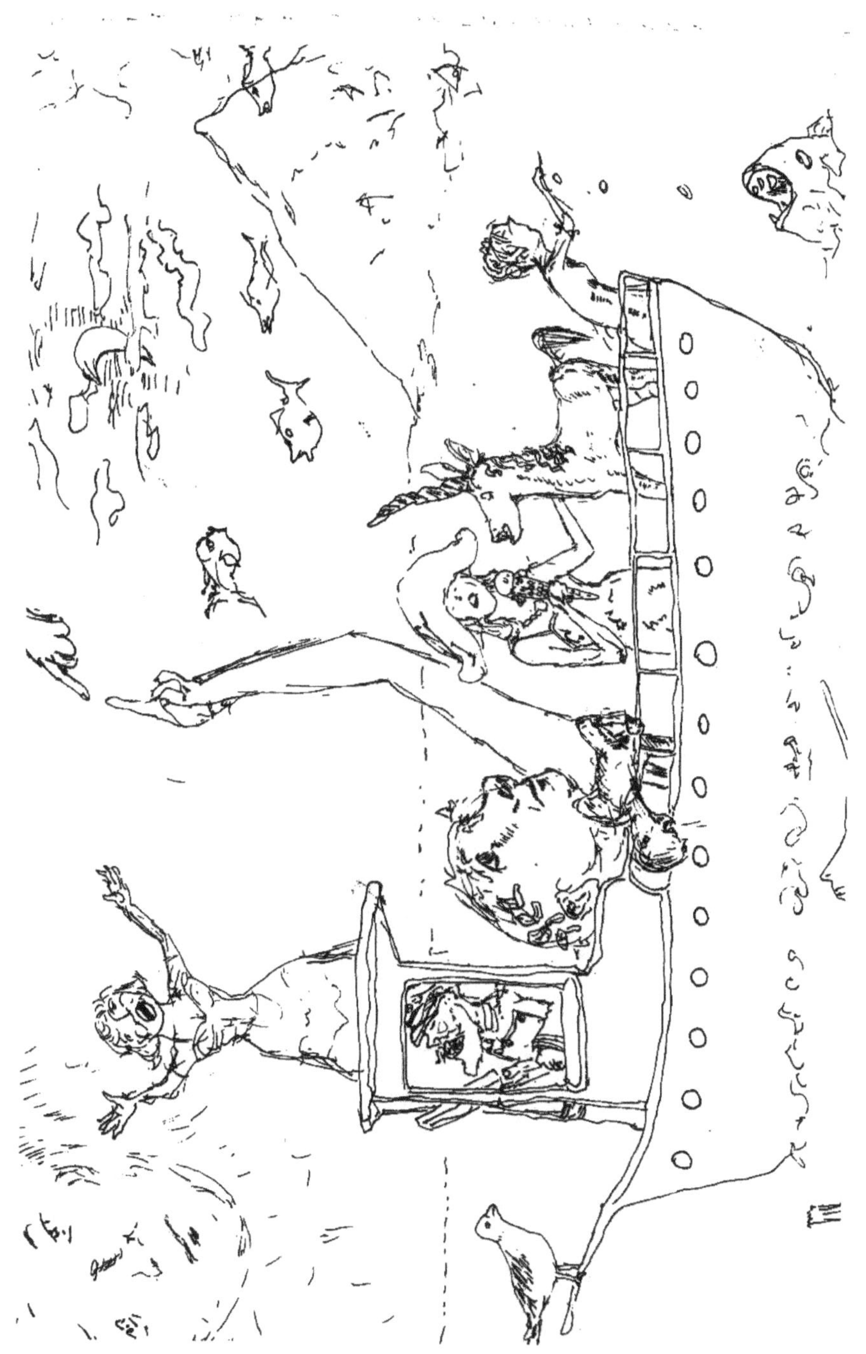

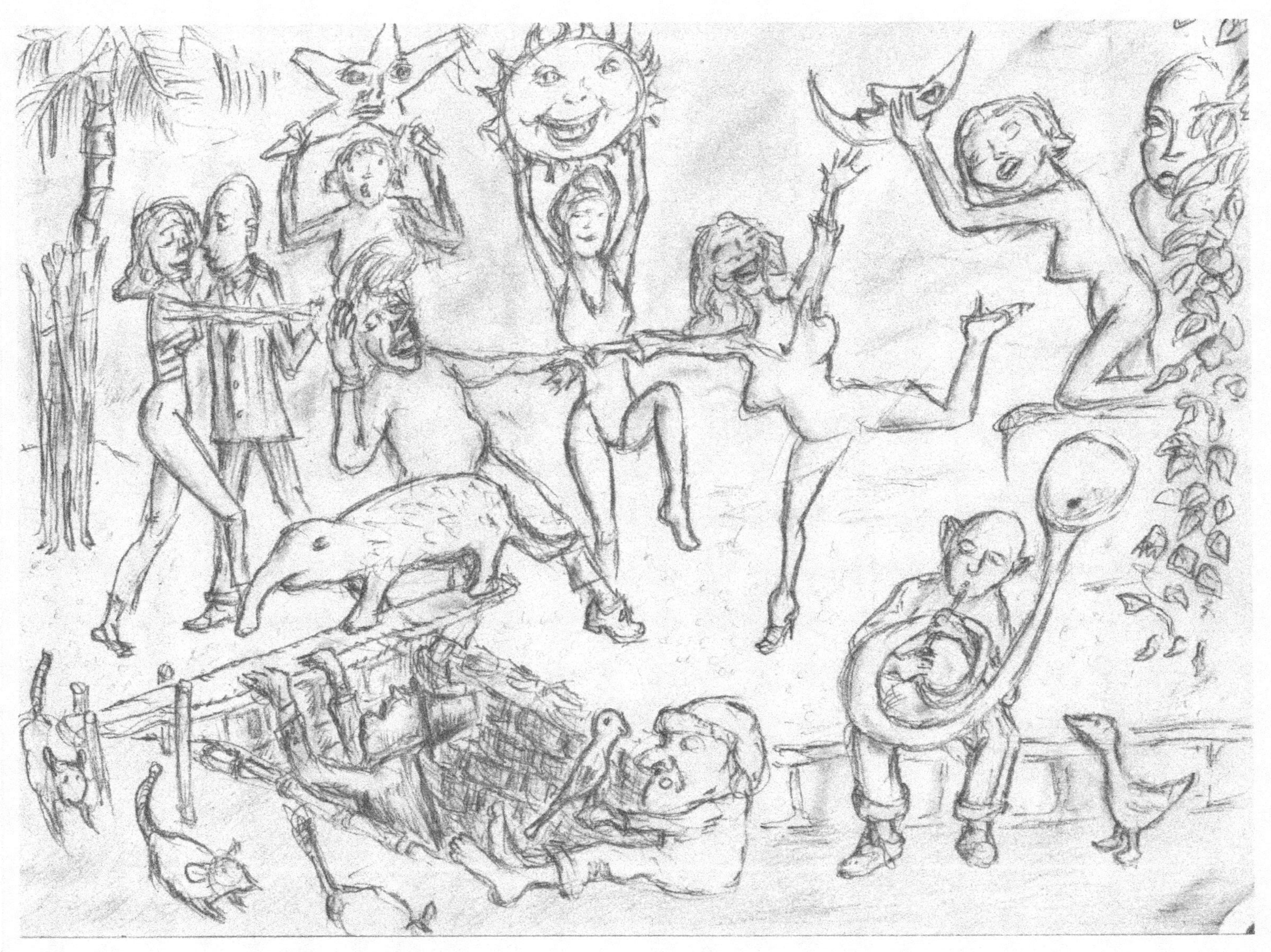

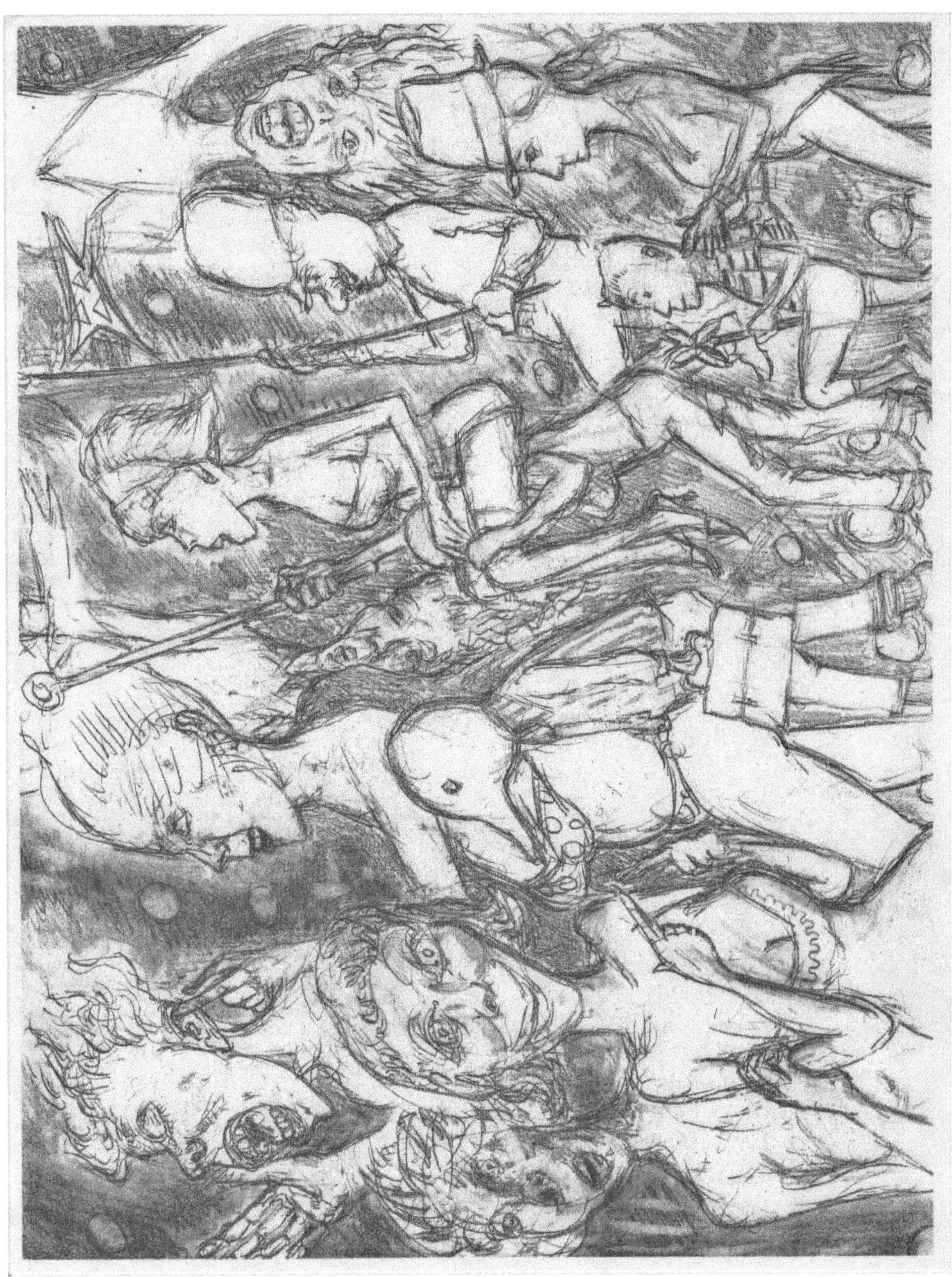

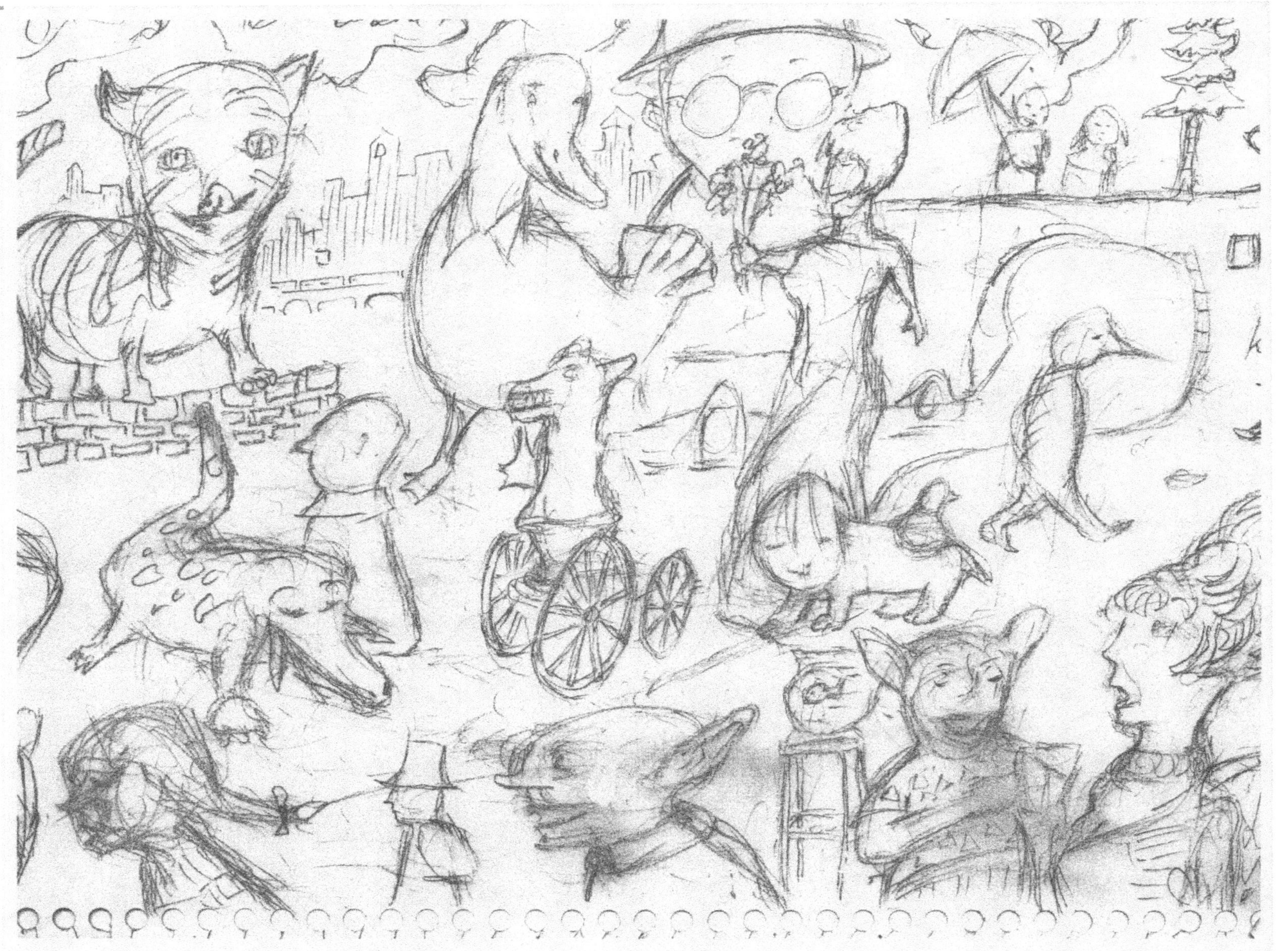

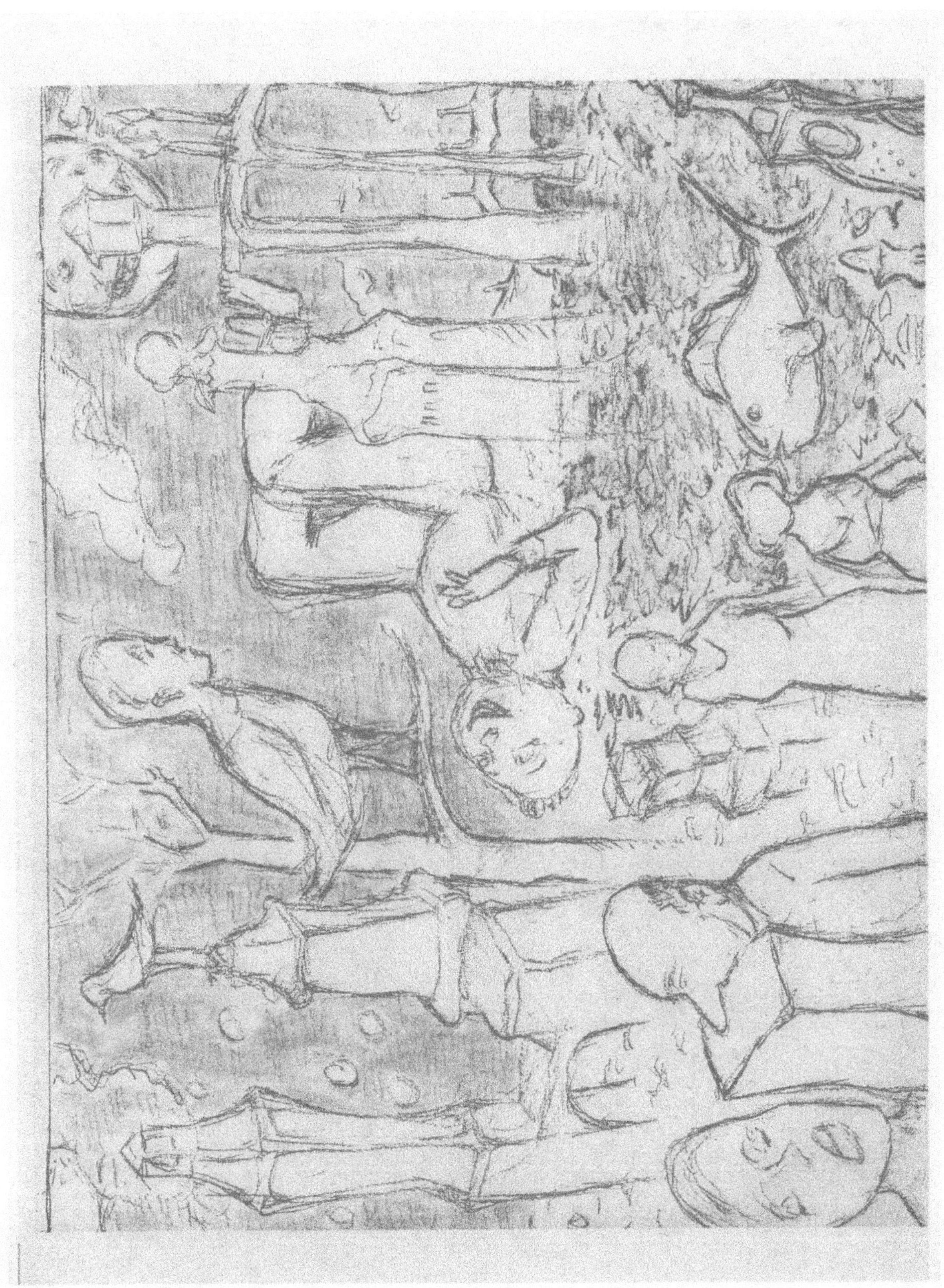

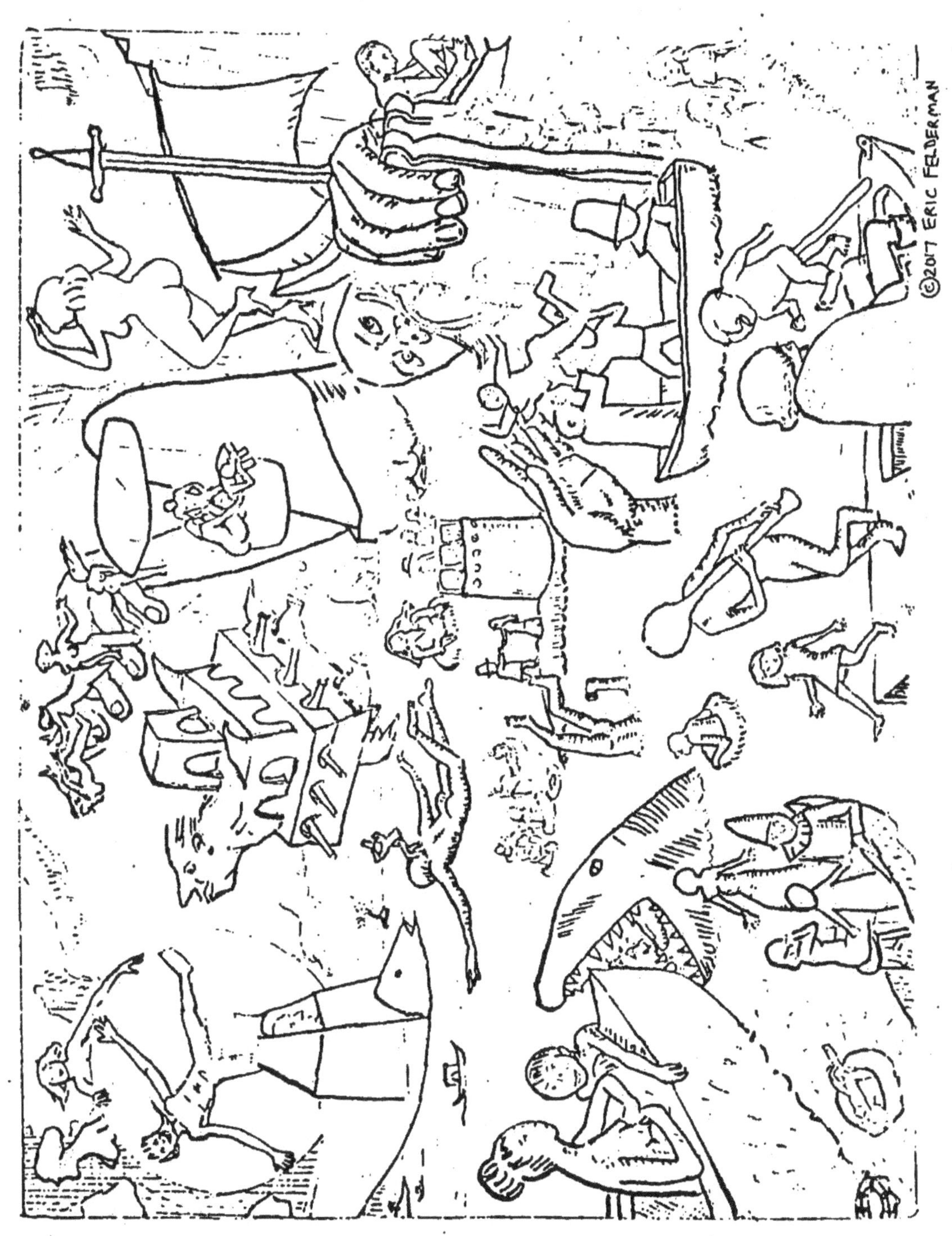

©2017 ERIC FELDERMAN

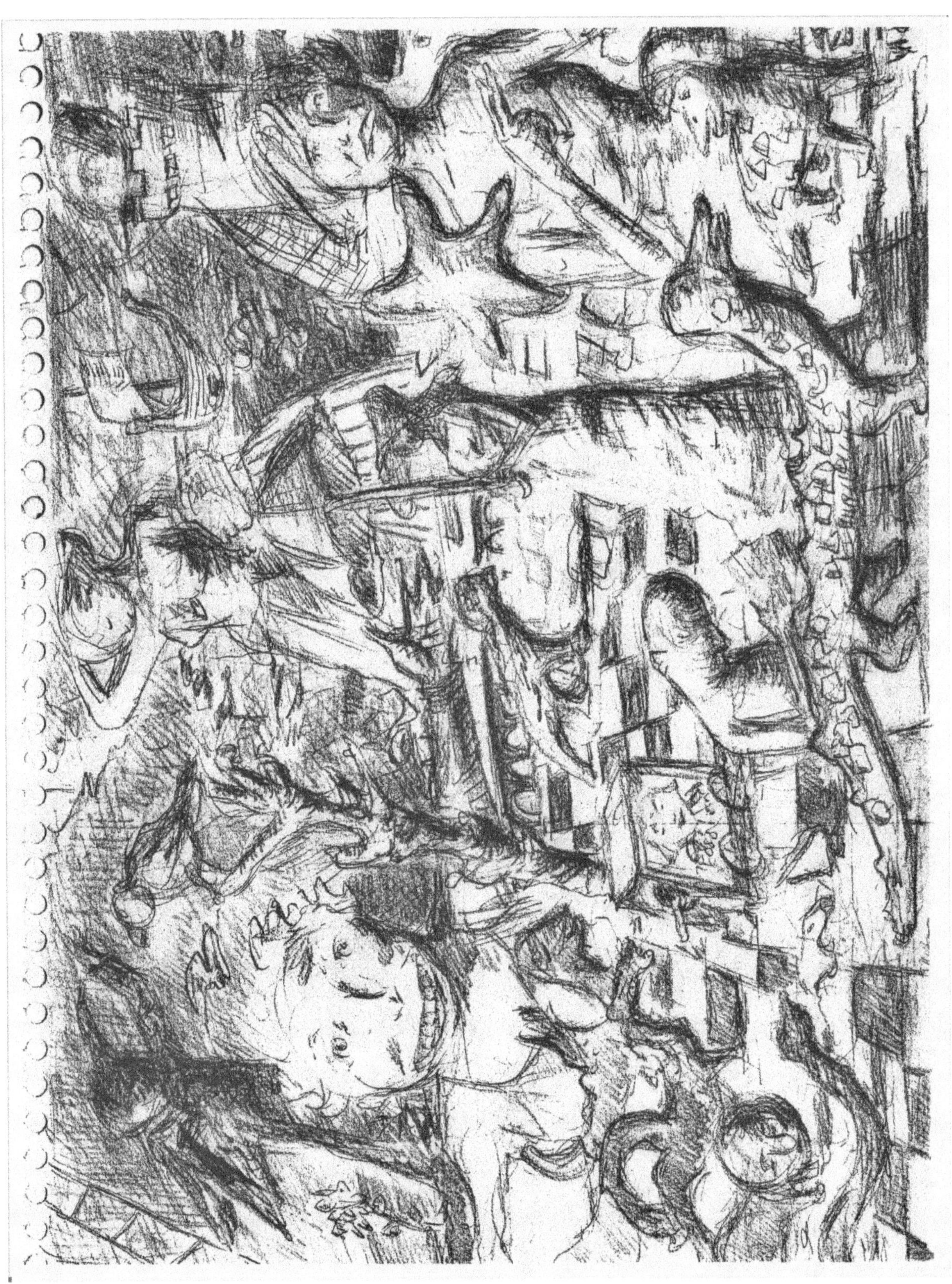

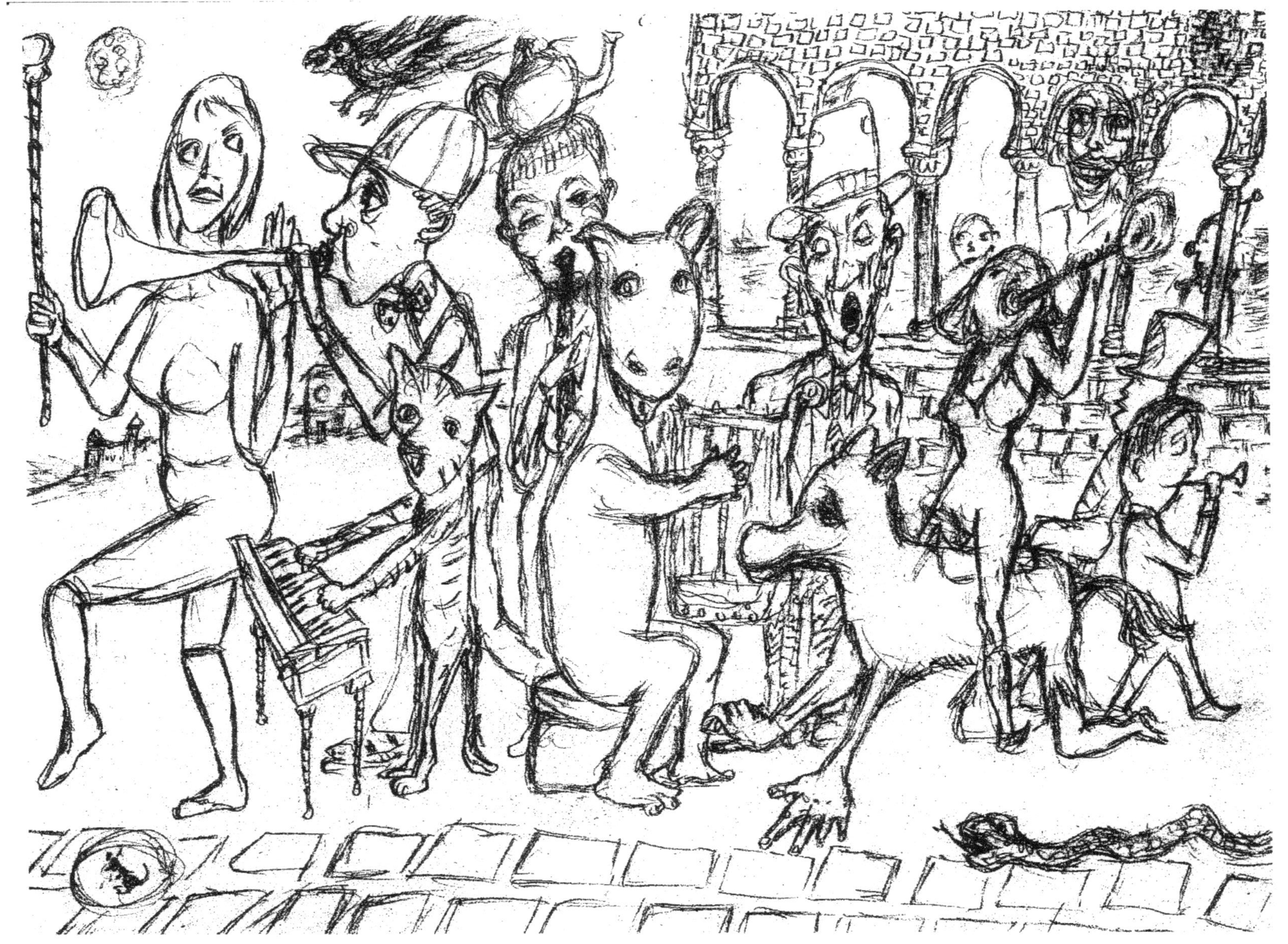

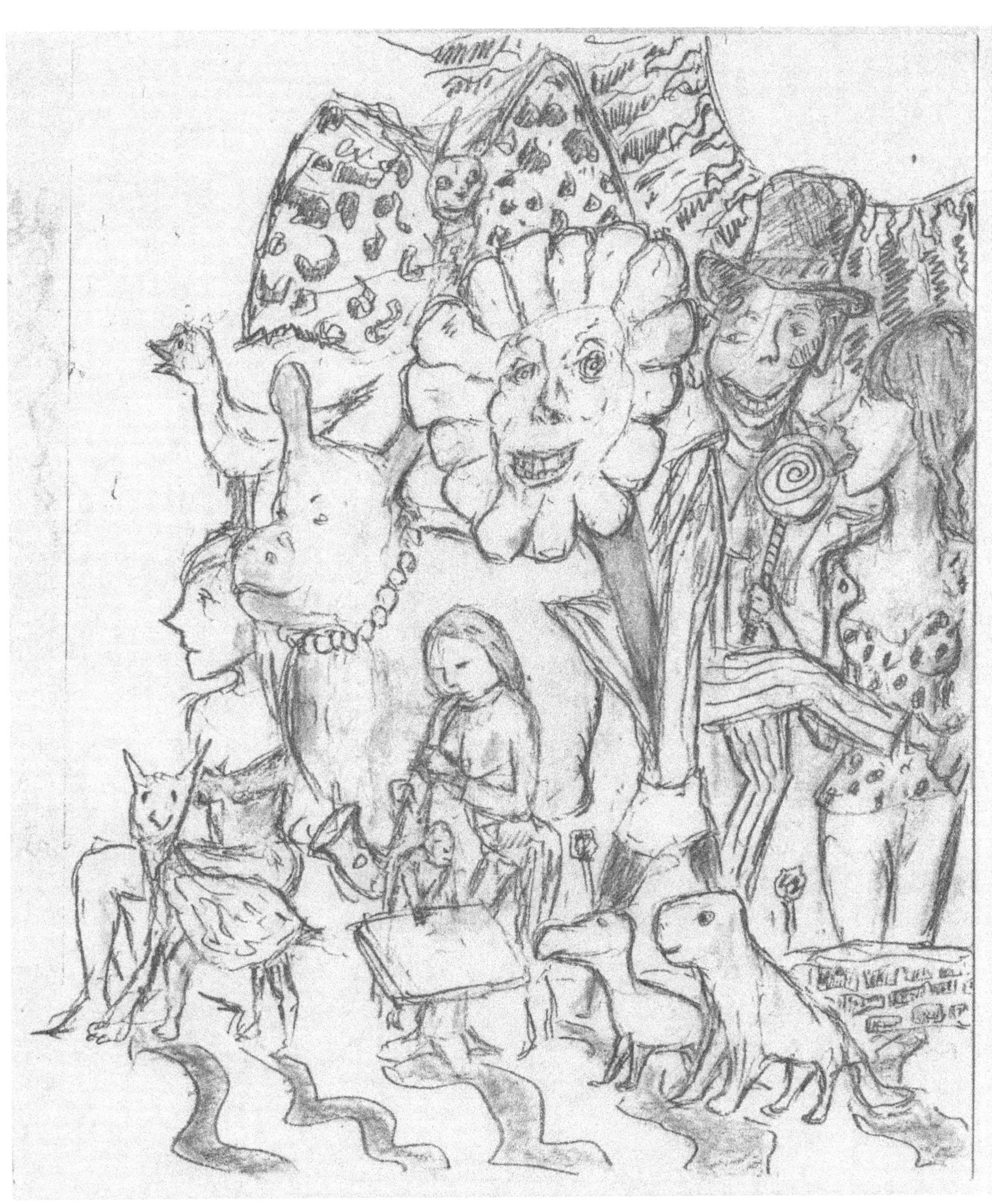

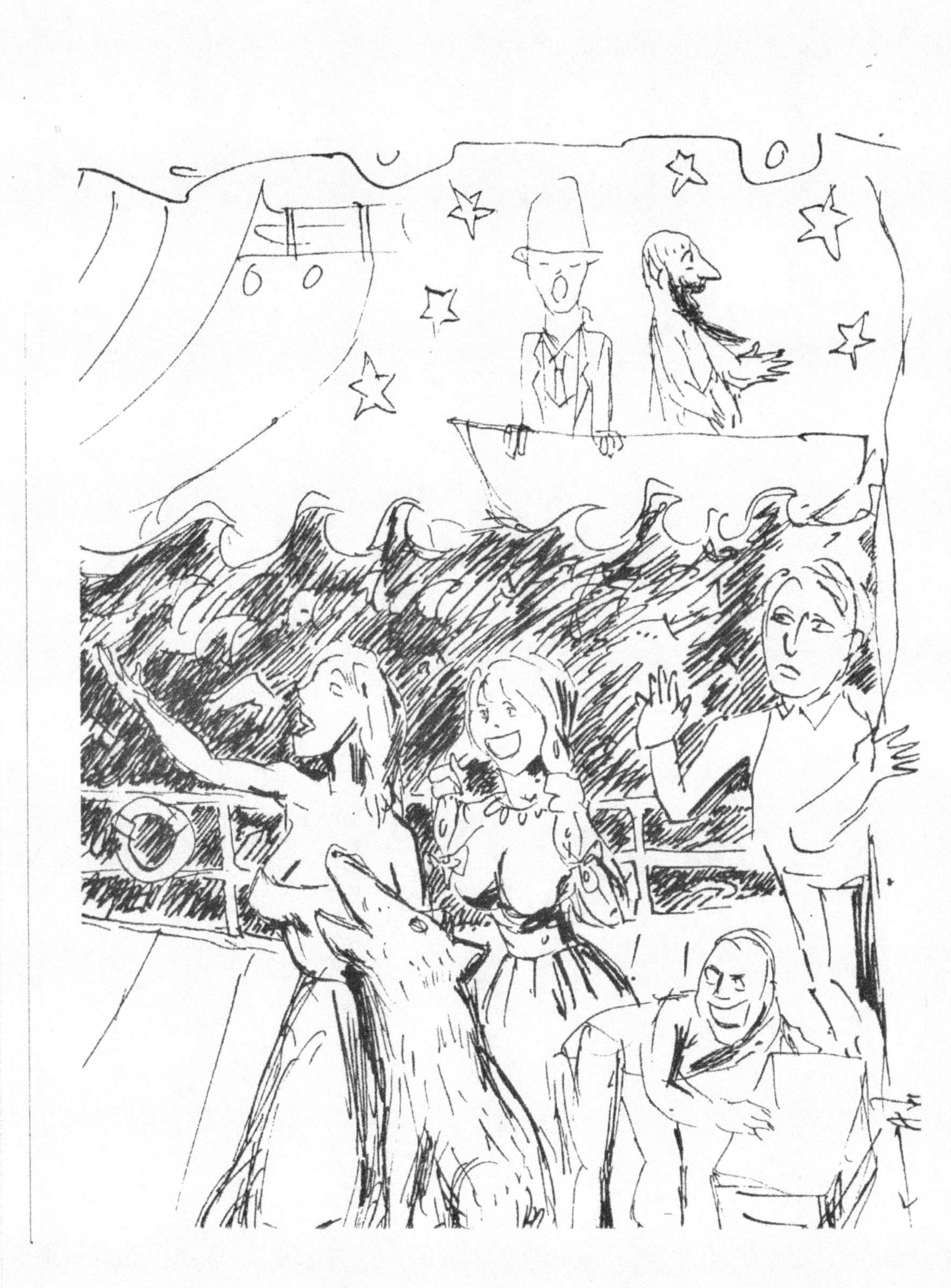

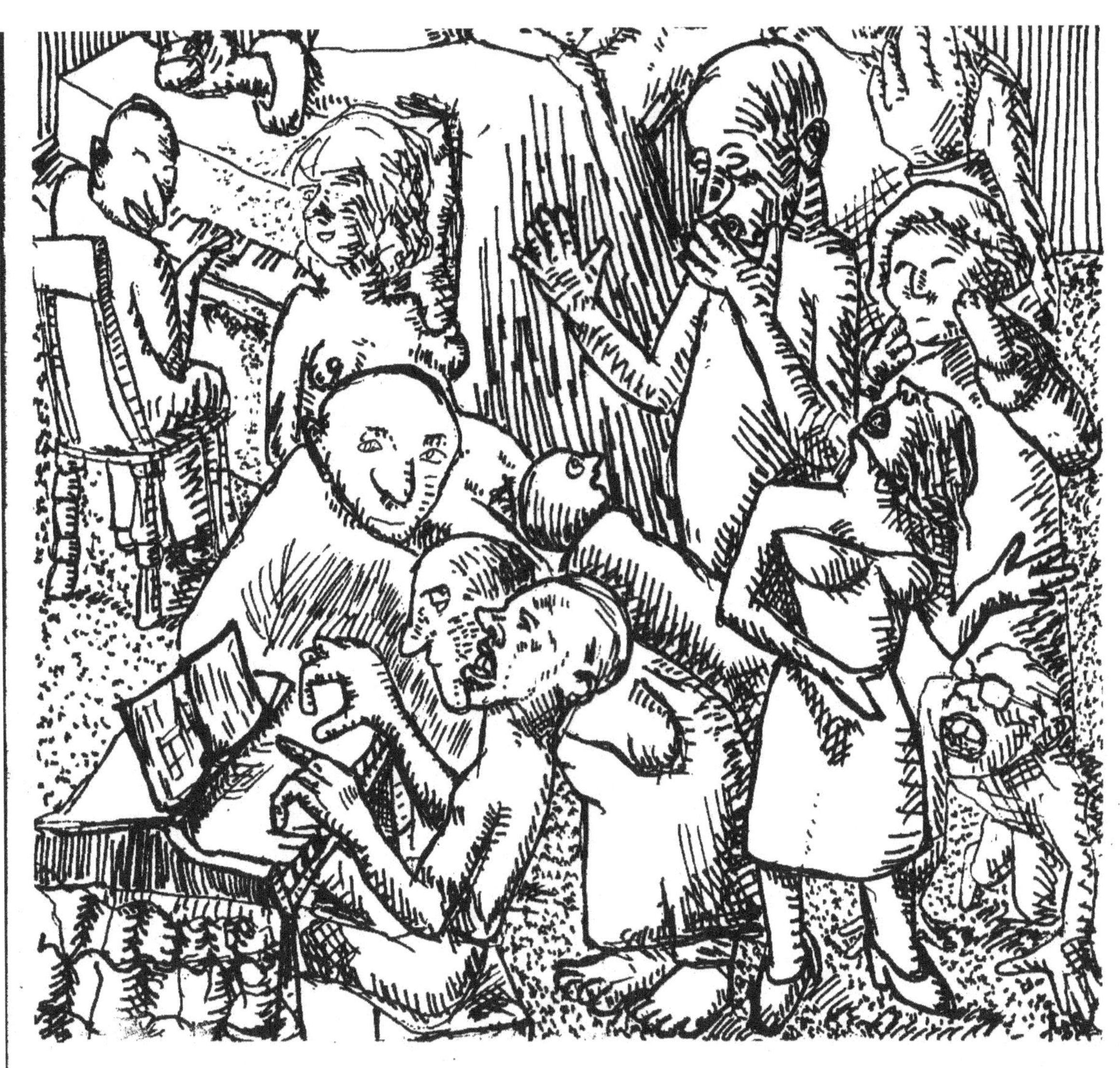

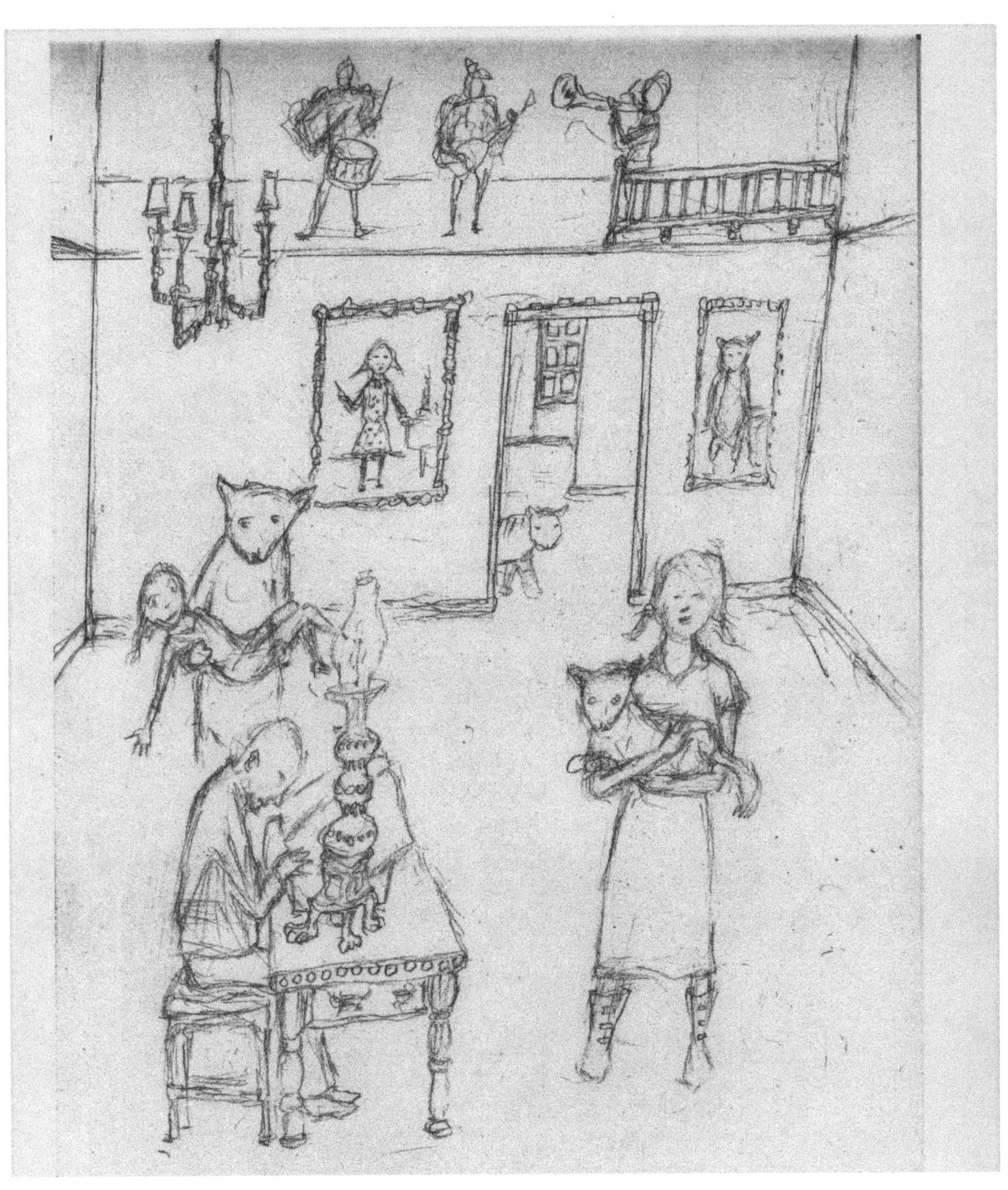

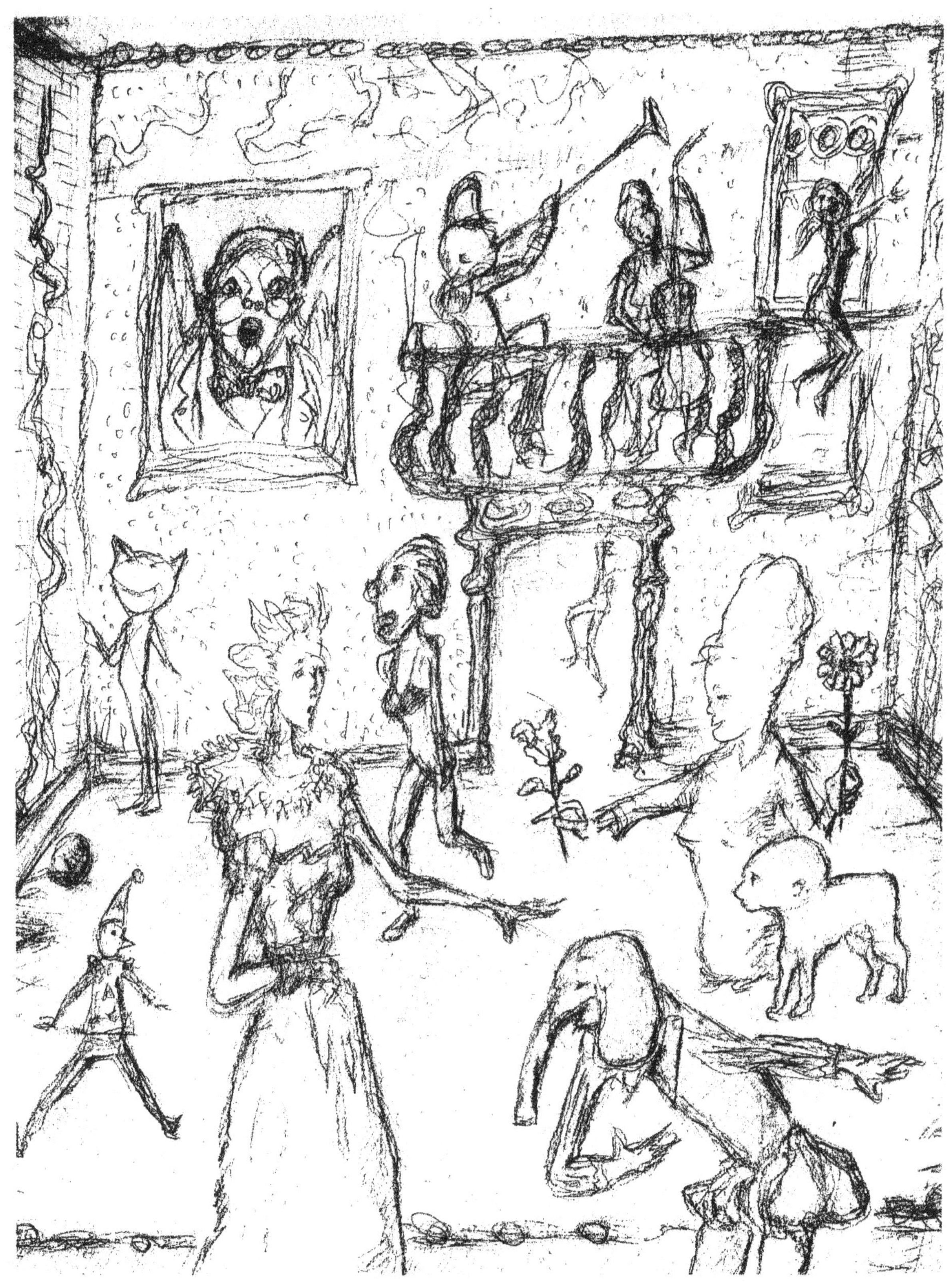

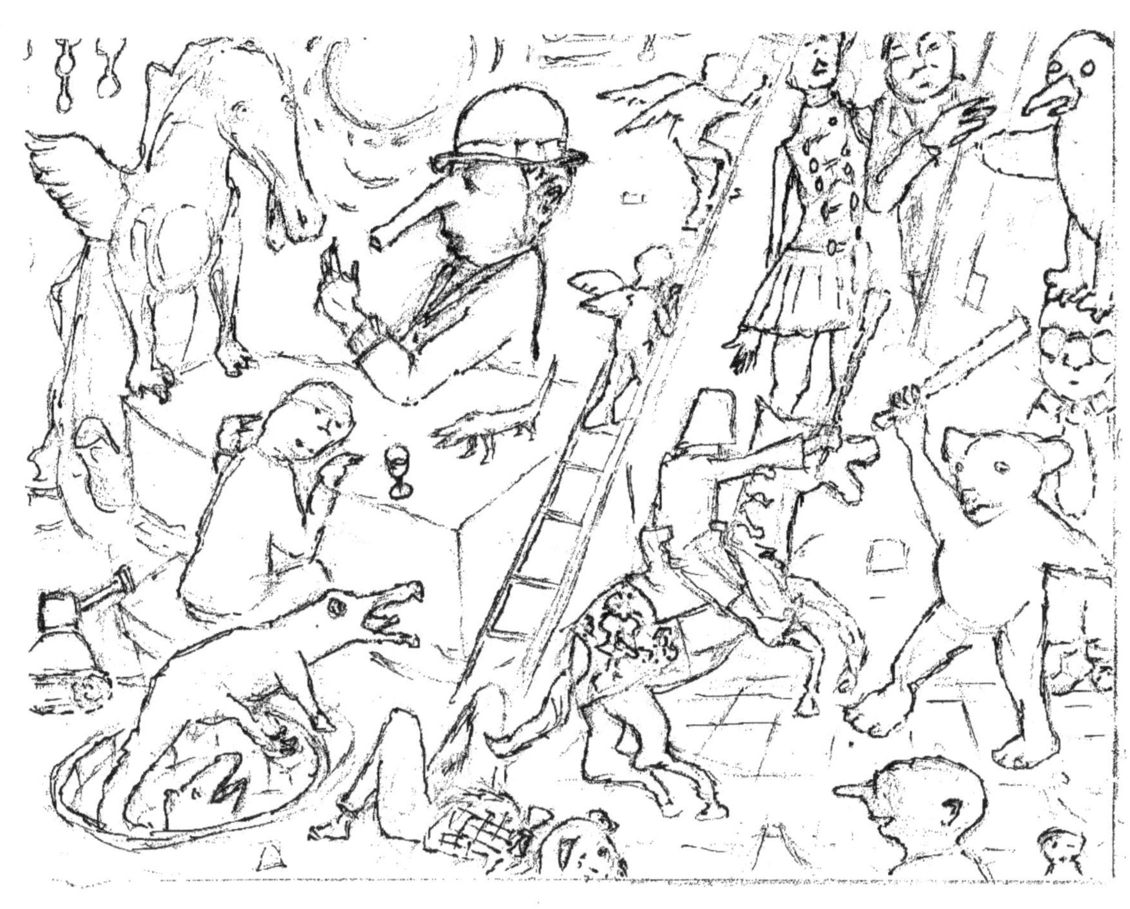

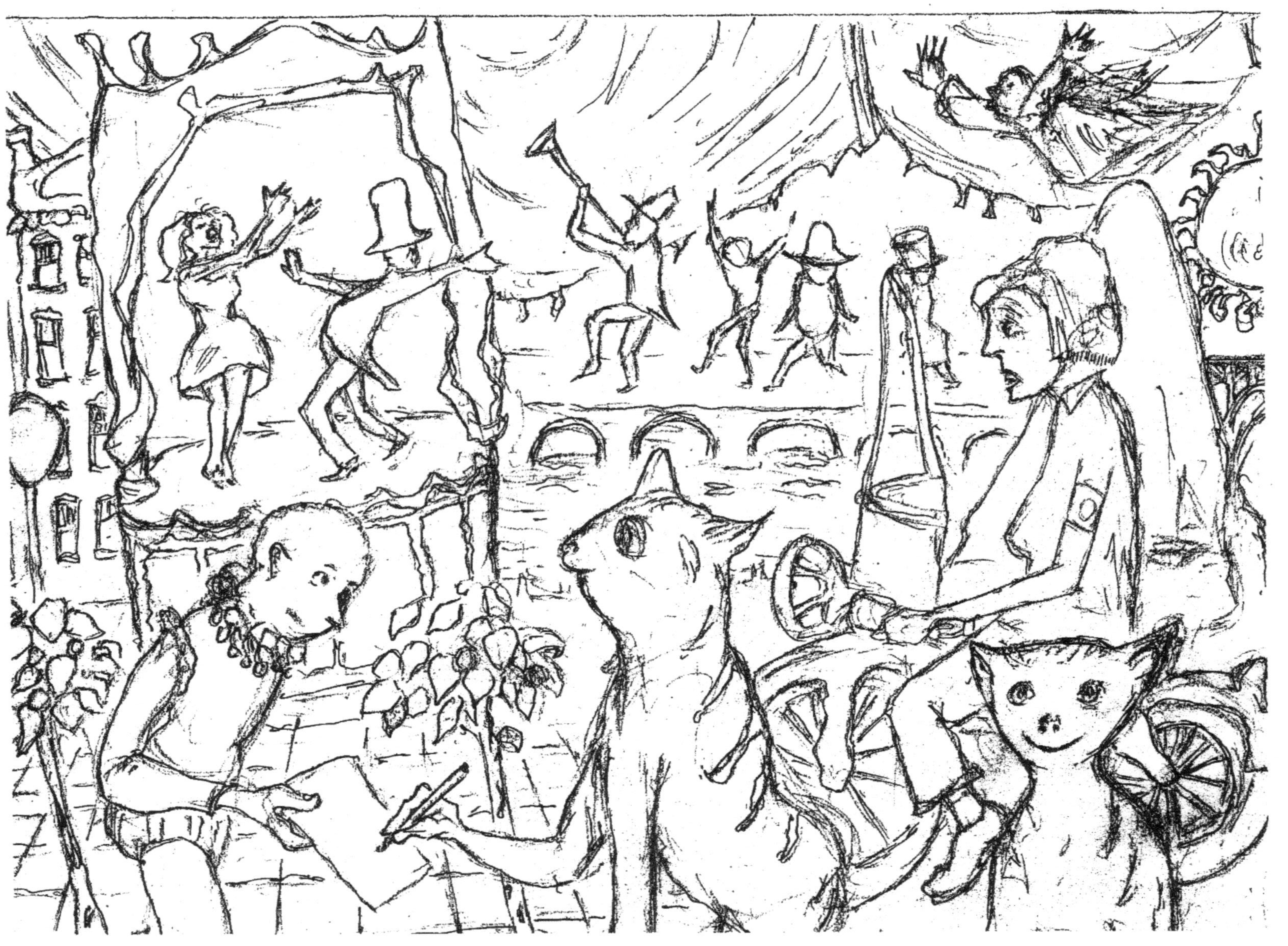

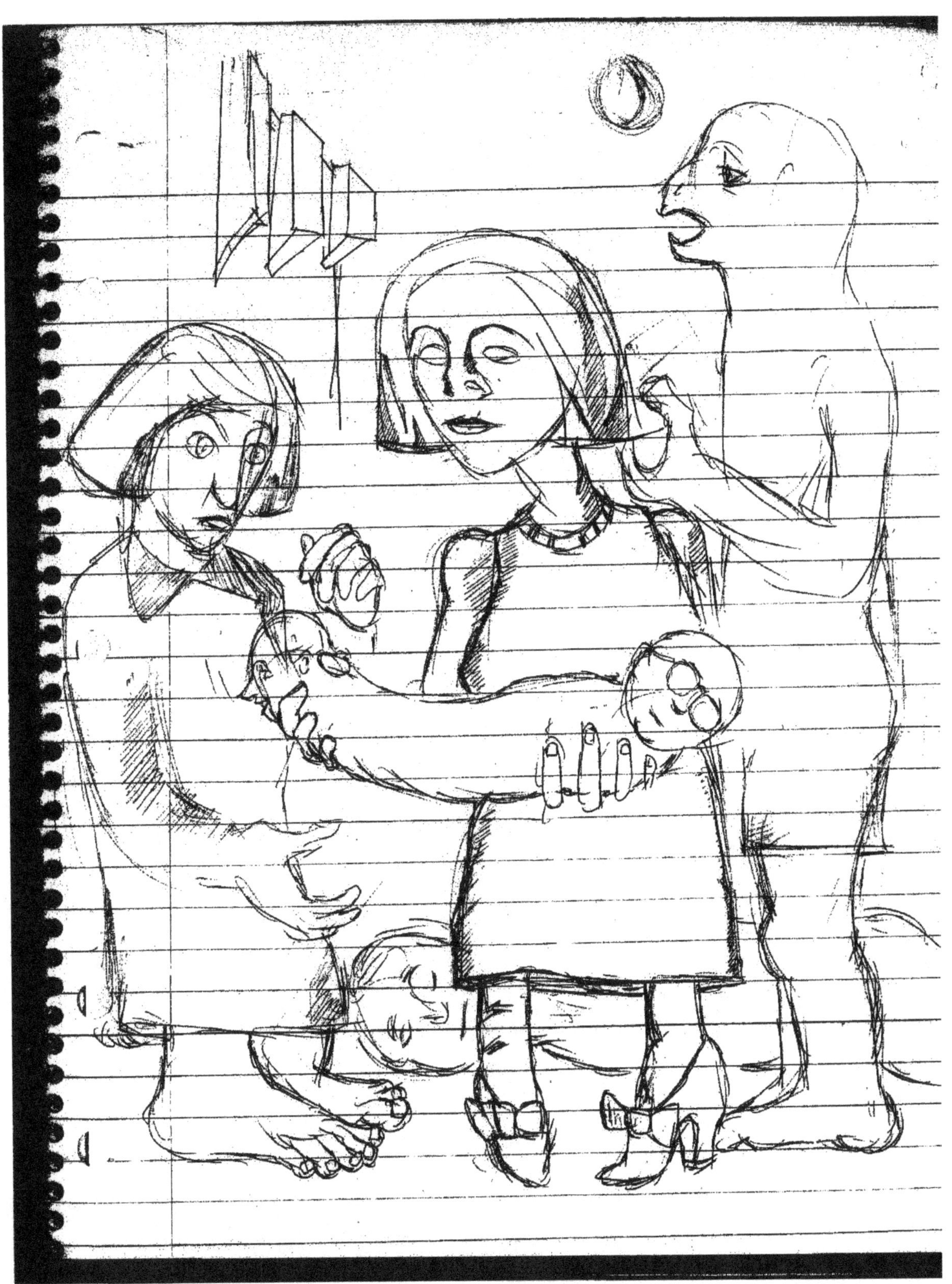

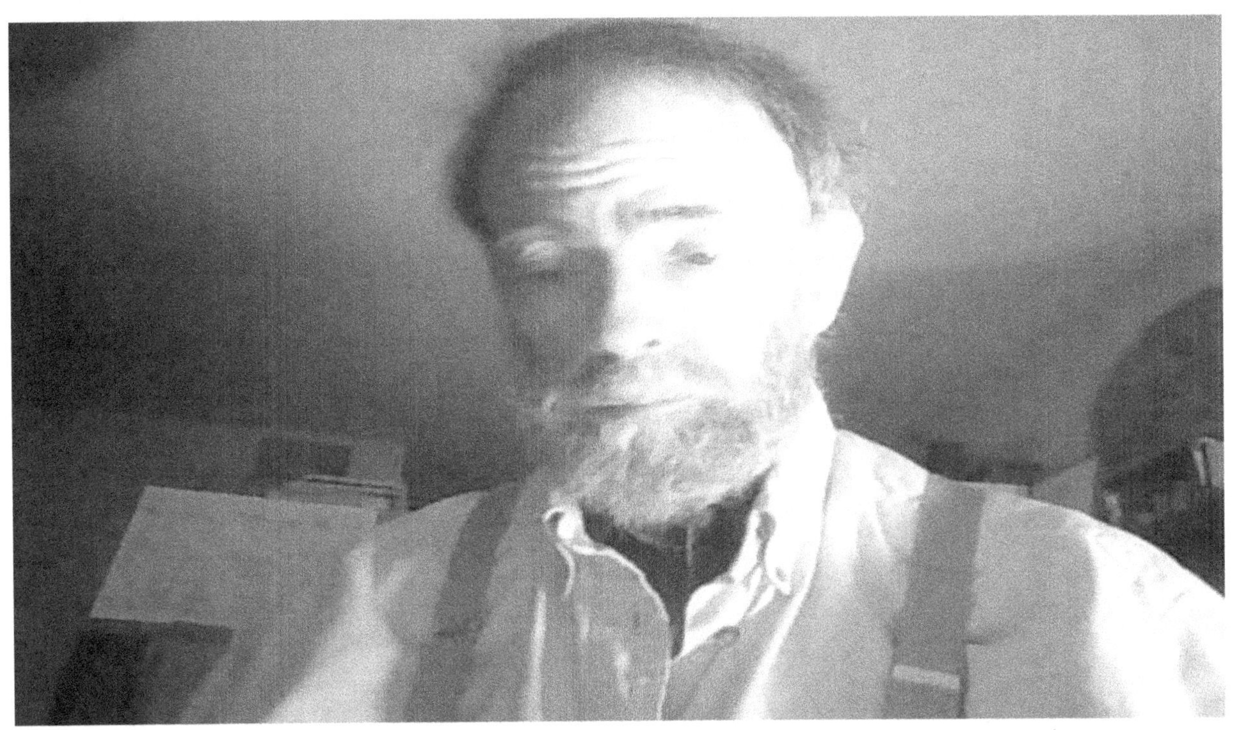